DR. MITESH PILLAI

DIGITAL HARMONY

Finding Balance in a Wired World

First Edition: March 2024
Printed in India

Printed at PrintPlus Pvt. Ltd., Mumbai.
Typeset in Adobe Garamond Pro

ISBN: 978-93-6070-984-6

Cover Design: Debabrata Sahoo

Publisher: StoryMirror Infotech Pvt. Ltd.
                  7th Floor, El Tara Building,
                  Behind Delphi Building,
                  Hiranandani Gardens,
                  Powai, Mumbai,
                  Maharashtra - 400076, India.

Web: storymirror.com
Facebook: @storymirror
Instagram: @storymirror
Twitter: @story_mirror
Contact Us: marketing@storymirror.com

Dedication

To my beloved spouse, whose unwavering support and understanding have been my guiding light throughout this journey. Your patience and encouragement have fuelled my passion for creating a better digital world.

To my dear mother and father, your boundless love and teachings instilled in me the values of empathy and perseverance. Your sacrifices inspire every step I take in advocating for mindful living.

To my cherished son and daughter, you are the motivation behind my commitment to shaping a balanced digital future. May this work contribute to a world where your generation thrives in harmony with technology.

And to my beloved country, India, with its rich heritage and ethos of unity in diversity. Your culture and spirit drive my dedication to nurturing a more balanced and mindful tech landscape for our nation's well-being.

Acknowledgments

Creating this book has been a collective endeavour, a symphony woven with the invaluable contributions of exceptional individuals.

Gratitude extends to the esteemed experts, psychologists, and professionals whose generosity in sharing wisdom and insights added depth and credibility to discussions about technology addiction and fostering mindful tech habits.

Special appreciation goes to those who bravely shared personal narratives. Your openness and vulnerability in recounting journeys toward balance and well-being in our digital world infused these pages with profound authenticity.

To my cherished family and friends: your unwavering support, enduring patience, and unwavering belief in this venture have formed the bedrock of this odyssey. Your encouragement fuelled my determination, and your understanding provided constant solace.

Lastly, to you, dear reader: your presence on this journey infuses vitality into the essence of this book. May these pages serve as guiding lights, illuminating pathways toward mindful boundaries in an ever-evolving digital landscape.

Thank you all for being instrumental in this profound and meaningful expedition.

Warm regards,

Dr. Mitesh Pillai

Preface

In the quiet hum of our digital age, amid the incessant buzz of notifications and the relentless march of progress, there exists a silent longing—a yearning for connection, for balance, and for a deeper understanding of ourselves within the vast web of technology that envelopes our lives.

As I pen these words, I am reminded of a timeless truth—a truth echoed through ancient scriptures and whispered through the ever-evolving corridors of time: "Vasudhaiva Kutumbakam"—the world is one family. This age-old wisdom holds a resonance that transcends generations and finds itself profoundly relevant in our digital era.

This book is born from a place of introspection, from the gentle whispers of shared experiences and the quiet struggles that unite us in our quest for balance amidst the ceaseless march of technology. It's a humble offering—a collection of thoughts, insights, and aspirations woven into the fabric of this digital age.

We stand at the precipice of an era where our devices connect us instantaneously, yet often leave us yearning for genuine connections. We navigate a landscape where screens have become windows to the world, blurring the lines between presence and absence, connection and isolation.

Through these pages, I invite you to join me on a deeply personal journey—one that transcends pixels and screens to delve into the essence of our shared humanity. It's a journey toward reclaiming balance, fostering mindfulness, and rediscovering the beauty of genuine connections in a world inundated with digital noise.

Here, in these words, I extend a hand—a hand that seeks to guide, to comfort, and to explore. Let us embark together, not merely as readers and author, but as kindred souls navigating the currents of an ever-evolving digital tapestry—a tapestry where our shared stories form the threads that bind us into the intricate, awe-inspiring fabric of "Vasudhaiva Kutumbakam."

May these words resonate with the beating of your heart, may they whisper truths that you've longed to hear, and may they pave a path toward a more balanced, mindful, and connected existence in this digital age.

With heartfelt gratitude and a shared journey ahead,

Dr. Mitesh Pillai

Contents

I.

Introduction to Technology Addiction

Chapter 1:

The Rise of Technology Dependency

1. Introduction

In an age defined by technological innovation, the world finds itself enveloped in a digital revolution, a metamorphosis driven by the rapid evolution of technology. The once-separate spheres of human existence and digital interconnectedness have seamlessly merged, reshaping the very essence of how individuals interact, work, and perceive the world around them.

This chapter serves as an exploration of the intricate landscape of our modern technological era. It is a journey that navigates through the profound and pervasive role that technology now plays in our lives—a role that transcends mere utility and has woven itself intricately into the very fabric of our existence.

Technological advancements once heralded for their promise of connectivity and efficiency, have morphed into agents of transformation, redefining industries, communication, and societal norms. From the nascent stages of computing to the advent of the internet and the ubiquitous presence of smartphones, our trajectory has been one of exponential growth and integration.

Industries across the spectrum have undergone a paradigm shift, embracing technological innovations to enhance productivity, streamline processes, and reshape the global economy. The convergence of automation, artificial intelligence, and big data has not only revolutionized work but has also redefined the contours of possibility, opening doors to realms once deemed unimaginable.

Simultaneously, the contours of interpersonal communication, once confined by geographic boundaries, have expanded exponentially. The digital realm has become an ecosystem teeming with real-time interactions, where distance holds little relevance, and information travels at the speed of light. These advancements have birthed a world of interconnectedness and access, promising boundless opportunities and global collaboration.

However, within this transformative landscape lies a subtler narrative—an evolving relationship, bordering on dependency, with the very tools designed to empower. The allure of seamless connectivity, addictive design elements of applications, and the perpetual quest for instant gratification have given rise to a complex interplay between humanity and technology.

This chapter endeavours to unpack the layers of this intricate relationship—the historical evolution, psychological underpinnings, societal shifts, and ethical considerations surrounding the rise of technology dependency. It seeks not only to understand the allure and impact of technological integration but also to navigate the path toward a harmonious and mindful coexistence with the digital realm.

As we embark on this exploration, it becomes evident that comprehending the roots of this dependency is paramount. By unravelling the complexities inherent in this relationship, we aim to pave the way for informed discussions and proactive measures, steering us toward a future where the symbiosis between humanity and technology fosters not dependency, but empowerment and enrichment.

2. Historical Evolution

The narrative of technological evolution echoes humanity's relentless pursuit of innovation, a journey that commenced with the clunky, room-sized computing machines of the mid-20th century, shrouded in scientific mystery and exclusive to specialized domains.

Embryonic Stages: Picture a time when computers occupied vast chambers, humming with the resonance of vacuum tubes and powered by punch cards. These pioneering machines, limited in computational capacity and accessible only to select scientific and military domains, laid the foundation for what would burgeon into a global digital revolution.

Revolutionary Strides: Progress unfurled with a torrent of transformative innovations—transistors replacing vacuum tubes, shrinking the behemoth machines into more manageable forms, and eventually birthing the integrated circuits that heralded a revolution in accessibility. Computing power, once the preserve of a select few, began its trajectory toward democratization.

The Internet's Genesis: Then, an invisible web, an interconnected ecosystem, emerged—the Internet. Initially conceived as a research network, it swiftly evolved into a global conduit of information and connectivity. Borders dissolved in this digital landscape, rendering geographical barriers irrelevant and opening the floodgates of global communication and information sharing.

Smartphone Revolution: Enter the epoch-defining era of smartphones. These sleek devices, empowered by computing capabilities dwarfing early mainframes, became extensions of our beings. With their touchscreens, omnipresent connectivity, and an arsenal of applications, they transformed from mere gadgets to indispensable companions, encapsulating our digital lives within their compact frames.

Impact on Society: The relentless march of technology left an indelible imprint on society. Industries metamorphosed, adapting to technological disruptions; communication transcended physical boundaries, connecting hearts and minds across continents; entertainment and information became accessible at the tap of a screen, reshaping how we entertain and inform ourselves.

Uncharted Frontiers: Yet, this journey is far from its conclusion. As we stand on the cusp of a new horizon, emerging technologies—artificial intelligence, quantum computing, and others—loom on the horizon. They whisper promises of innovation yet unseen, of landscapes yet unexplored, propelling us towards a future brimming with possibilities and uncharted territories.

Legacy of Progress: The legacy of technological evolution is not merely in its gadgets or machines but in its profound impact on human lives. It's a narrative of progress, a testament to humanity's boundless ingenuity and the transformative power of innovation.

3. Technological Advancements and Dependency

In the tapestry of technological evolution, an intriguing narrative emerges—a story not merely of innovation but of an intricate relationship, bordering on dependency, between humanity and the digital realm. This section endeavours to peel back the layers of this symbiotic yet complex relationship, unveiling the psychological and societal factors that underpin the burgeoning dependency on technology.

The Psychology of Addiction: At the heart of technology dependency lies a tapestry of psychological triggers meticulously woven into the design of certain applications, social media platforms, and immersive gaming experiences. These digital landscapes are crafted not merely for utility but with an intent to captivate, enthral, and retain user attention. From the intermittent rewards of notifications to the infinite scroll of content, these digital environments are structured to create a continuous loop of engagement, fostering a sense of compulsion and dependency.

Design for Engagement: Consider the captivating allure of social media platforms—an intricate labyrinth of likes, shares, and comments. Each interaction triggers a surge of dopamine, the brain's pleasure-inducing neurotransmitter, fostering an addictive cycle. Similarly, gaming experiences, with their rewarding mechanisms and immersive narratives, can lure individuals into prolonged engagements, creating a sense of dependency and craving for continued interaction.

Attention Economy: In the landscape of the attention economy, where user engagement equates to success, tech companies leverage persuasive design elements to prolong user interactions. Techniques like infinite scrolling, personalized recommendations, and push notifications act as digital hooks, ensnaring attention and fostering a cycle of habitual usage.

Societal Implications: The ramifications of technology dependency extend beyond individual psychology to societal dynamics. A society interconnected through digital platforms grapples with altered social norms, communication patterns, and perceptions of reality. The ubiquitous nature of technology blurs the lines between virtual and physical existence, presenting a conundrum wherein the quest for digital connectivity sometimes supersedes genuine human interaction, leading to societal shifts in interpersonal relationships and communication.

Striking a Balance: While technology brings forth unparalleled convenience and connectivity, the fine line between utility and dependency necessitates a delicate balance. Understanding the psychological mechanisms behind the addictive design is pivotal in fostering mindfulness and informed usage. It calls for a nuanced approach that acknowledges the allure of technology while empowering individuals to navigate its landscapes mindfully.

4. Impact on Daily Life: Embracing the Digital Revolution

The heartbeat of modern existence pulsates with the rhythm of technology, orchestrating a symphony that permeates every facet of daily life. From the confines of the workplace to the corridors of education, and from the interwoven threads of social interactions to the tapestry of entertainment, technology's omnipresence has ushered in a revolution— altering landscapes, redefining norms, and leaving an indelible imprint on humanity's daily narrative.

The Digital Workspace: Imagine stepping into the bustling realm of the modern workplace—a convergence of technological marvels that orchestrate productivity. From cloud-based collaboration to seamless communication tools, the digital landscape amplifies efficiency, transforming how tasks are executed and collaborations are forged. Yet, in this digital symphony, the boundary between professional dedication and personal life blurs—a dance that demands a mindful equilibrium.

Education Reimagined: In the halls of education, technology has wielded its transformative wand. Digital textbooks, interactive learning platforms, and virtual classrooms have shattered geographical barriers, offering a smorgasbord of educational possibilities. Yet, within this digital renaissance, the question of equitable access to educational resources echoes—a reminder of the divide that technology can perpetuate.

Redefined Social Interactions: The panorama of social interactions paints a picture of interconnectedness—a tapestry woven by social media platforms, messaging apps, and virtual communities. The ability to bridge distances and maintain connections across continents enriches human relationships. However, lurking beneath this digital connectivity lies a paradox—the dichotomy between virtual connectedness and genuine, face-to-face human encounters.

Entertainment in the Digital Age: Entertainment, once confined to theatres and television screens, now resides within handheld devices. Streaming services, gaming realms, and social media platforms offer a cornucopia of entertainment choices at the tap of a screen. Yet, the immersive nature of digital entertainment unveils concerns—questions about excessive screen time, sedentary lifestyles, and the allure of escapism within virtual realms.

The Pendulum Swings: Technology, a double-edged sword, wields both promise and peril. While it bestows unparalleled convenience and connectivity, it dances perilously close to the edge of overreliance. The very tools designed for efficiency can become conduits of distraction, blurring the lines between work and leisure. The ceaseless deluge of information raises alarms about digital inundation and its impact on mental well-being.

Seeking Harmony: Amidst this digital whirlwind, the pursuit of balance emerges as an anthem—a resonating call for mindful navigation. Embracing the conveniences of technology while guarding against its potential pitfalls becomes an art. It beckons individuals to unplug, to forge genuine human connections, and to discern when to embrace the digital wave, and when to retreat for moments of rejuvenation.

5. Statistics and Research: Unveiling the Global Tapestry of Technology Dependency

In the vast digital expanse that defines our contemporary world, statistical revelations serve as guiding stars, illuminating the contours of a society deeply intertwined with technology. These empirical insights peel back the layers, offering a compelling narrative of the prevalence and ramifications of technology dependency—providing not just figures but a reflection of our digital zeitgeist.

Global Penetration: The canvas of technology dependency spans continents and cultures, weaving a ubiquitous presence that transcends geographical borders. Statistics gleaned from comprehensive research unveil a staggering embrace of digital devices worldwide. From the bustling metropolises to the remotest corners, technology has woven itself into the fabric of human existence.

Excessive Screen Time: At the heart of this digital revolution lies a concerning revelation—excessive screen time has become the emblem of our technological era. Research studies, spanning diverse age cohorts, spotlight an entrenched engagement with screens. The allure of digital interfaces—be it smartphones, tablets, or computers—engulfs individuals, reshaping daily routines and leisure pursuits.

Age and Adherence: Statistical analyses paint a nuanced portrait of technology dependency across age brackets. The digital natives, nurtured in an era awash with technology, exhibit heightened screen engagement, seamlessly integrating devices into their lives. Yet, paradoxically, older demographics—once deemed less inclined towards technology—also showcase an increased affinity for digital interfaces, blurring generational demarcations.

Demographic Realities: Beyond age, the statistical landscape unravels the tapestry of dependency shaped by demographic nuances. Socioeconomic disparities, cultural contexts, and geographic variations forge divergent paths in screen engagement. These variations in access, literacy, and cultural attitudes manifest in disparate screen time habits across populations.

Projections and Imperatives: Statistical insights not only chronicle the present but also cast shadows on future trajectories. They forecast a world further enmeshed in technology, raising concerns about the potential repercussions of sustained excessive screen time on mental well-being, physical health, and societal dynamics.

Provoking Change: Armed with these compelling statistics, the narrative extends beyond mere observation—it becomes a catalyst for action. The statistics, while emblematic of our digital era, propel discussions, policies, and interventions aimed at fostering mindful engagement. They illuminate the urgency for informed dialogues and initiatives that navigate the path toward a more balanced, purposeful coexistence with technology.

6. Cultural and Societal Shifts: The Digital Evolution Unveiled

Step into the captivating whirlwind of the digital age—a realm where technology acts as a catalyst, reshaping the very fabric of our cultural tapestry. Here, within the labyrinth of digital connectivity, lie profound transformations in communication, social norms, and the intricate threads that weave our relationships.

An Evolution in Communication: Imagine a landscape where conversations are condensed into snippets, where emojis convey emotions, and where virtual platforms transcend borders. This digital revolution reshapes the nuances of communication, birthing a language unique to the online realm. The brevity of text and the immediacy of responses redefine the art of expression, painting a canvas where words transcend physical limitations.

Norms Transformed: As the digital era unfolds, so do the norms of society. Virtual lives intertwine with physical identities, blurring boundaries once considered sacrosanct. The notion of privacy transforms, riding the waves of online sharing and the perennial balancing act between revealing and concealing aspects of one's life.

The Tapestry of Relationships: Within the digital web, families find themselves navigating new dynamics. Screens infiltrate domestic spaces, altering the dynamics of familial bonding. Conversations transcend physical proximity, but questions arise about the depth of these digital connections and their impact on traditional familial rituals.

Friendships in the Cyber Age: Friendship extends its wings beyond geographical confines. The digital sphere births friendships across continents, creating global networks tethered by pixels and shared interests. Yet, amidst this vast expanse, the yearning for deeper connections persists, hinting at the dichotomy between virtual companionship and tangible intimacy.

The Strain of Perpetual Connectivity: Enter the world of 'always-on' connectivity, where the borders between work and personal life blur incessantly. Digital devices beckon, creating an unending loop of accessibility. The allure of constant connection clashes with the need for respite, sparking a tug-of-war between productivity and burnout.

Harmony Amidst the Digital Storm: Amidst this whirlwind of change, a quest for equilibrium emerges. It's a journey—a pursuit to reconcile the convenience of digital connection with the authenticity of human interaction. It's about carving out sanctuaries where genuine connections thrive amidst the noise, nurturing relationships that transcend the confines of screens.

7. Ethical Considerations: The Moral Frontier of Technology

Step into the ethical labyrinth that lies at the heart of our digital evolution—a landscape where technology intersects with moral boundaries, stirring contemplation on the ethical tapestry woven by our digital dependency. This conclusion ventures into the uncharted terrain of ethical quandaries—privacy, data commodification, and the ethical obligations vested in those crafting the addictive allure of digital products.

Preserving the Veil of Privacy: In the digital realm, the notion of privacy becomes an enigma—a treasure to safeguard amidst the encroaching shadows of surveillance. As technology permeates every facet of existence, questions of personal sanctity linger. The battle between convenience and privacy beckons, evoking profound reflections on the sanctity of personal space in an era of perpetual connectivity.

Data as Currency, Ethics as Stewardship: Personal data, a currency bartered in the digital marketplace, raises ethical spectres. The commodification of this invaluable asset raises ethical dilemmas—questions about its ethical acquisition, utilization, and the implicit ethical responsibility to protect this treasure trove from exploitation and manipulation.

The Moral Compass of Tech Entities: Within the digital domain, tech companies wield immense power—a power entwined with ethical responsibilities. The creation of addictive products raises ethical queries. The deliberate design elements that captivate attention and foster dependency necessitate a revaluation of ethical boundaries, echoing the imperative for ethical design and transparent practices.

Forging an Ethical Path: Concluding this discourse on technology dependency, the clarion call for ethical innovation reverberates. It's a call to architects of technology to navigate the digital landscape guided by ethical frameworks. It's an impassioned plea to craft a future where innovation thrives in harmony with ethical stewardship—a future where technology enriches lives without compromising ethical standards.

8. Key Takeaways: Navigating the Realm of Technology Dependency

As we conclude this chapter, a tapestry of insights emerges, offering a panoramic view of our symbiotic relationship with technology. This chapter serves as a compass, guiding us through the intricate maze of technology dependency while laying the cornerstone for deeper exploration in subsequent chapters.

Integration into Modern Life: Technology, once a tool, has metamorphosed into an inseparable companion—a silent confidant threading through the fabric of modern existence. Its omnipresence in work, education, social interactions, and entertainment underscores its pervasive integration into our daily routines.

Escalating Dependency: Within this digital odyssey lies a burgeoning dependency—a subtle intertwining of humanity with the allure of technology. The allure of screens, addictive design elements, and the ever-expanding digital landscape contribute to an escalating dependency, reshaping behaviours and societal norms.

A Call for Understanding: This chapter unveils the need for a profound understanding of the roots of technology dependency. It's a clarion call—a recognition that unravelling the psychological, societal, and ethical intricacies underpinning dependency is pivotal in crafting effective prevention and intervention strategies.

Foundation for Exploration: As this chapter draws to a close, it serves as a foundational pillar—a scaffold upon which subsequent chapters will scaffold. It lays bare the complexities of our digital journey, urging further exploration into the multifaceted dimensions of technology dependency.

Prelude to Action: The stage is set—a stage that beckons us to delve deeper into the realms of psychological effects, societal ramifications, ethical considerations, and the pursuit of balance. It's an invitation to explore strategies, interventions, and mindful approaches that navigate the labyrinth of technology dependency.

In essence, this chapter provides a comprehensive overview—a panorama unveiling the pervasive integration of technology into modern life and serves as a springboard for profound exploration—a journey to unravel the roots of dependency in pursuit of strategies that foster a harmonious coexistence with technology.

Chapter 2:

Understanding Addiction in a Digital Age

1. Introduction: Unveiling Addiction in the Digital Epoch

Step into a realm where the boundaries between habit and compulsion blur—a landscape where the tendrils of addiction weave a complex narrative within the tapestry of the digital era. This chapter unfurls the canvas of addiction in its nuanced interplay with technology, setting the stage for a profound exploration of its mechanisms and manifestations.

The Shifting Facets of Addiction: Addiction, a term resonating with historical connotations, undergoes a metamorphosis in the digital age. No longer confined to substances, addiction transmutes into an intricate web entwined with digital interfaces. It encompasses not only substances but also behaviours, sparking a paradigm shift in our understanding of addictive tendencies.

Digital Lures and Allure: Within this digital panorama lie lures crafted to captivate—a symphony of algorithms, design elements, and psychological triggers meticulously woven into the fabric of technology. These digital siren songs beckon, engendering habitual behaviours and fostering dependencies that mirror traditional addiction patterns.

Understanding the Mechanisms: Addiction in the digital epoch operates through intricate mechanisms, intertwining psychological, neurological, and behavioural facets. It's a labyrinth where reward circuits are hijacked, habituation thrives, and the fine line between use and abuse blurs—an exploration that requires delving into the depths of human cognition and behaviour.

Unmasking Manifestations: The manifestations of digital addiction, though subtler than traditional dependencies, imprint themselves on daily routines and mental landscapes. Excessive screen time, compulsive social media checking, and gaming immersion are but a few facets of this multifaceted addiction, leaving indelible imprints on individual behaviours.

Embarking on a Deeper Exploration: As this chapter unfurls the introductory curtains, it beckons readers to traverse deeper into the labyrinth of addiction in the digital age. It's an invitation—a voyage of exploration to decipher the underlying mechanisms, the nuanced manifestations, and the transformative insights paving the way for a mindful coexistence with technology.

2. Defining Addiction in the Digital Landscape: Unravelling Complex Behaviours

Within the digital landscape lies an intricate web—a confluence where human behaviours intertwine with technology, birthing a nuanced understanding of addiction. This section navigates through the labyrinth of addiction's nature, elucidating its manifestations in the realm of technology while debunking misconceptions and delineating the fine line between habitual use and addiction.

Complex Behavioural Patterns: Addiction, a tapestry of complex behaviours, transcends the traditional confines of substance dependency in the digital epoch. It metamorphoses into a spectrum of habits and compulsions, threading its way through excessive screen time, compulsive social media engagement, gaming immersion, and other behaviours fostered by technology's allure.

Misconceptions and Clarifications: Amidst the digital deluge, misconceptions shroud the understanding of addiction. It's imperative to delineate the nuances—an addiction to technology does not solely hinge on the substance but on behavioural patterns. It's the compulsive engagement, the inability to cease despite adverse consequences, that defines this digital dependency.

Habitual Use vs. Addiction: The dichotomy between habitual use and addiction emerges as a focal point. Habitual use, a routine engagement with technology, might be a norm in the digital era. However, addiction transcends this—it's an all-encompassing compulsion, a state where technology usurps control, dictating behaviours and disrupting daily life.

The Shifting Paradigm: As technology burgeons, the parameters of addiction blur. It's not merely the hours spent glued to screens but the intricate psychological underpinnings that define addiction. This exploration illuminates the evolution of addiction—how it adapts to the digital milieu, reshaping behavioural norms and posing challenges in identifying its thresholds.

The clarity for Informed Navigation: As misconceptions dissipate, clarity emerges—an understanding that addiction in the digital age is a mosaic of behaviours intricately entwined with technology. It's a clarion call for informed navigation, a pathway illuminated by discernment, fostering a landscape where users tread mindfully amidst the digital allure.

3. Neuroscience and Technology Addiction: Unveiling the Brain's Response

Enter the enigmatic realm of neuroscience—a landscape where the intricate dance of technology and the brain's reward system unfolds. This section navigates through the neurological corridors, elucidating how technology intricately triggers the brain's reward mechanisms, delving into the release of dopamine, and unravelling the neurological impact of prolonged engagement in digital activities such as screen time, gaming, and social media.

The Dopaminergic Symphony: At the heart of addiction lies a symphony conducted by neurotransmitters, prominently dopamine. Technology, with its compelling allure, orchestrates a surge in dopamine release—an activation akin to traditional addictive substances. Prolonged engagement fuels this dopaminergic surge, fostering a cycle of dependence and craving.

Screen Time and Dopamine: The allure of screens intertwines with the brain's reward circuitry. Every notification, scroll, or victory in digital realms triggers a dopamine surge—a gratification that fuels habitual screen engagement. This cycle perpetuates, reinforcing the neural pathways associated with digital stimuli.

Gaming and Social Media Impact: The digital landscape burgeons with immersive experiences—be it gaming realms or the social arenas of social media. Both domains propel the release of dopamine, offering rewards, validations, or accomplishments, creating a neurological landscape ripe for addictive tendencies.

Neuroplasticity and Habituation: Prolonged exposure to digital stimuli remodels the brain's architecture—an aspect governed by neuroplasticity. The incessant engagement rewires neural pathways, fostering habituation. This process fuels the propensity for continued digital engagement, contributing to the entrenchment of addictive behaviours.

Implications for behavioural Patterns: Understanding the neurological impact of technology unveils profound implications for behavioural patterns. The dopamine-driven cycle of reward and craving underlines the mechanisms behind addictive behaviours in the digital realm, fostering a realization of the neurological entanglement between technology and the human brain.

4. Behavioural Psychology and Technology Use: Unveiling Compulsive Behaviours

Step into the realm of behavioural psychology—a domain where the intricacies of human behaviours interlace with the allure of technology. This section delves into behavioural psychology's lenses, examining reinforcement schedules, habit formation, and the intricate psychological drivers that underpin compulsive device use in the digital era.

Reinforcement Schedules: Within the digital landscape lie carefully crafted reinforcement schedules—an orchestration of rewards that fuel habitual engagement. Variable rewards, notifications, likes, or in-game achievements follow intermittent schedules, fostering a cycle of anticipation, engagement, and gratification that perpetuates habitual device use.

Habit Formation in the Digital Realm: Habits, forged by repetition, find fertile ground in the digital milieu. The constant engagement with screens etches neural pathways, birthing habitual behaviours. As actions become routine, the interplay between cues, routines, and rewards forms a cycle that cements compulsive device use within daily routines.

Psychological Drivers of Compulsion: Compulsive device use unravels the psychological drivers that underpin behaviours. The fear of missing out (FOMO), social validation, or the comfort derived from digital escapism act as psychological anchors fostering continued engagement. These drivers perpetuate habitual behaviours, entwining individuals deeper into the digital embrace.

Operant Conditioning and Digital Engagement: The principles of operant conditioning, deeply entrenched in the digital landscape, propel behaviours. Positive reinforcements amplify engagement—every click, like, or interaction serves as reinforcement, solidifying the behavioural loop and intensifying the compulsion to remain connected.

Breaking the Cycle: Understanding behavioural psychology offers insights into breaking the cycle of compulsive device use. Interventions focusing on altering reinforcement schedules, restructuring habits, and addressing underlying psychological motivators become pivotal in fostering mindful technology engagement.

5. Risk Factors and Vulnerabilities: Unveiling Contributors to Technology Addiction

Amidst the digital panorama, a multitude of factors converges, shaping vulnerabilities and paving the path to technology addiction. This section elucidates diverse risk factors that intertwine and contribute to the propensity for addictive behaviours in the digital realm, encompassing age, personality traits, underlying mental health conditions, social environments, and accessibility to technology.

Age as a Contributing Factor: The developmental stages of life serve as a lens through which technology addiction manifests. Adolescents and young adults, amidst identity formation and peer influence, exhibit heightened susceptibility to addictive behaviours due to the malleability of their evolving neural networks.

Personality Traits and Propensities: Individual personality traits weave a tapestry of susceptibilities. Traits such as impulsivity, sensation-seeking, and low self-esteem act as catalysts, amplifying the proclivity for engaging in excessive digital activities, and nurturing the seeds of addiction.

Underlying Mental Health Conditions: The intricate relationship between mental health and technology addiction emerges. Conditions like depression, anxiety, or attention-deficit hyperactivity disorder (ADHD) serve as fertile ground for addictive behaviours, offering a refuge within the digital realm, and exacerbating vulnerabilities.

Social Environments and Influences: The social fabric weaves a complex narrative, fostering either resilience or susceptibility to addiction. Peer dynamics, familial influences, or societal norms shape behaviours—nurturing either healthy tech habits or perpetuating patterns of excessive engagement.

Accessibility and Exposure to Technology: The omnipresence and accessibility of technology in daily life create an environment ripe for addictive behaviours. Unrestricted access, coupled with a digital landscape designed for engagement, heightens the susceptibility to prolonged and compulsive device use.

Intersection of Multiple Factors: It's the intricate interplay between these risk factors—a convergence of age, personality, mental health, social environments, and accessibility—that culminates in an individual's susceptibility to technology addiction, creating a multifaceted landscape of vulnerabilities.

6. **Understanding the Spectrum of Addiction: Unveiling Varied Manifestations**

Within the digital labyrinth lies a spectrum—a continuum

where technology addiction manifests in diverse hues, ranging from mild preoccupation to severe dependency. This segment peer into the multifaceted landscape of addictive behaviours, exploring how addiction spans across individuals, unfurling different degrees of engagement and potential escalations.

Mild Obsession and Preoccupation: At the lower echelon of the spectrum lies mild obsession—a realm where engagement with technology exceeds normal patterns yet remains within manageable bounds. It manifests as frequent checking, an elevated interest, or a habitual engagement that doesn't significantly impair daily functioning.

Moderate Engagement and Emerging Dependency: Moving along the spectrum, moderate engagement unveils deeper entrenchment. Here, technology assumes a more central role, encroaching further into daily routines. The behaviours intensify—extended screen time, increased social media usage, or escalating gaming immersion—showing signs of dependency but with manageable disruptions.

Severe Dependency and Escalating Behaviours: Towards the higher end of the spectrum resides severe dependency—an abyss where technology usurps control, dictating behaviours and impairing daily functioning. Here, the compulsions intensify, overshadowing real-life engagements, and leading to social isolation, academic or work impairments, and psychological distress.

Individualized Manifestations: Addiction, a mosaic of behaviours, unfurls differently across individuals. What constitutes mild obsession for one might manifest as severe dependency for another. The spectrum acknowledges the individualized nature of addictive behaviours, embracing the diversity of manifestations.

Escalation and Intervention: The spectrum hints at the potential escalation of addictive behaviours—a trajectory where mild obsessions might burgeon into severe dependencies if left unchecked. It underscores the imperative for timely interventions, emphasizing the need for awareness, detection, and tailored strategies to mitigate the escalation of addictive behaviours.

7. Social and Cultural Influences: Unveiling the Acceptance of Excessive Technology Use

Amidst the tapestry of societal constructs, norms, and cultural dynamics, lies a landscape sculpted by societal norms, peer influences, and cultural trends—a terrain that shapes the perceptions and acceptance of excessive technology use. This analysis delves into the intricate web of influences, elucidating how societal constructs foster the normalization and acceptance of extensive engagement with technology.

Societal Norms and Shifting Perceptions: Societal norms wield immense power, dictating acceptable behaviours within communities. The digital era witnesses a paradigm shift—what was once deemed excessive screen time is gradually normalized, and embraced as a societal norm propelled by the ubiquitous integration of technology into daily life.

Peer Pressure and Social Validation: Peer dynamics, an influential force, shape attitudes and behaviours toward technology use. The pursuit of social validation, acceptance, and conformity within peer groups fosters a culture where excessive digital engagement garners admiration rather than concern, perpetuating the normalization of prolonged screen time or constant connectivity.

Cultural Trends and Technological Utopia: Cultures paint a canvas where technological advancements are glorified—a symbol of progress and modernity. Cultural trends often exalt the virtues of constant connectivity, framing it as a gateway to success, knowledge, and social standing, further embedding the normalization of extensive technology use.

The Reinforcement Loop: Within this societal framework, a reinforcement loop emerges—a cycle where societal norms, peer influences, and cultural trends fuel each other. The normalization of excessive technology use perpetuates societal acceptance, fostering a landscape where digital immersion becomes synonymous with social assimilation.

Impact on Perception and Intervention: Understanding these social and cultural influences offers insights into perceptions and interventions. It underscores the importance of challenging norms, reshaping cultural trends, and fostering critical conversations to shift societal perceptions—creating an environment conducive to mindful and balanced technology engagement.

8. Recognizing the Signs and Symptoms: Unveiling the Telltale Indicators

Within the intricate tapestry of technology dependency lies a myriad of indicators—subtle whispers hinting at a struggle beneath the surface. This section serves as a guide, offering insights into identifying behavioural, emotional, and physical signs signalling potential technology addiction.

Behavioural Indicators:

- Excessive Screen Time: Prolonged and uninterrupted engagement with digital devices, surpassing normal usage patterns.

- Escapism: Using technology as a means of escaping real-life challenges or unpleasant emotions.

- Neglecting Responsibilities: Prioritizing digital engagement over essential tasks like work, education, or personal responsibilities.

- Withdrawal Symptoms: Irritability, restlessness, or agitation when unable to access digital devices or networks.

Emotional Indicators:

- Anxiety or Distress: Experiencing heightened anxiety when not engaged with technology or when trying to cut down usage.

- Dependence on Digital Validation: Seeking constant validation, likes, or comments on social media for emotional fulfilment.

- Mood Swings: Fluctuations in mood accompanied by digital engagement or its restriction.

Physical Indicators:

- Physical Discomfort: Headaches, eye strain, or musculoskeletal issues due to prolonged screen time.

- Sleep Disturbances: Disrupted sleep patterns attributed to late-night screen usage or compulsive engagement.

- Fatigue and Irritability: Feeling fatigued or irritable after extended periods of screen use.

Interconnectedness of Indicators: It's vital to note that these signs often interconnect, painting a holistic picture of potential technology addiction. An individual may exhibit a combination of these signs, indicating a deeper struggle with excessive digital engagement.

Importance of Awareness and Intervention: Recognizing these signs and symptoms becomes pivotal. It empowers individuals and caregivers to intervene timely, fostering an environment conducive to seeking help and implementing strategies for mindful technology engagement.

9. Impact on Mental Health and Well-being: Unveiling Psychological Consequences

Within the digital domain lies a shadow—a realm where excessive engagement casts a profound impact on mental health and well-being. This segment delves into the intricate interplay, elucidating the psychological consequences stemming from technology addiction, including anxiety, depression, social withdrawal, and a myriad of other mental health ramifications.

Anxiety and Heightened Stress: Prolonged digital engagement seeds anxiety—a constant need for connectivity, the fear of missing out (FOMO), and the anticipation of notifications induce stress, fostering an anxious mindset that permeates offline life.

Depression and Emotional Turmoil: Excessive digital immersion often shadows emotional well-being. Feelings of inadequacy, comparison-induced dissatisfaction, or the relentless pursuit of validation contribute to a downward spiral into depressive states, impacting self-esteem and mental health.

Social Withdrawal and Isolation: The allure of digital realms can foster social withdrawal. As individuals gravitate towards screens, real-life interactions diminish, leading to a sense of isolation, disconnectedness, and a decline in social relationships, further exacerbating mental health concerns.

Sleep Disturbances and Fatigue: The impact extends beyond psychological realms—disrupted sleep patterns due to late-night screen engagement or compulsive device use result in fatigue, affecting overall well-being and cognitive functioning.

Cognitive Impairments and Attentional Deficits: Prolonged exposure to screens disrupts attentional capacities—fragmented attention spans, reduced concentration, and cognitive impairments become prevalent, impacting academic, professional, and personal spheres.

Vicious Cycle of Mental Health Impact: These consequences intertwine, fueling a vicious cycle—mental health ramifications induce increased digital escapism, perpetuating the very behaviors that exacerbate psychological distress.

The Imperative for Intervention and Support: Understanding the profound impact of technology addiction on mental health underscores the urgency for intervention. It emphasizes the need for support structures, mindfulness strategies, and therapeutic interventions aimed at restoring mental well-being amidst the digital deluge.

10. Key Takeaways: Navigating the Landscape of Technology Addiction

1. Comprehensive Understanding of Addiction Mechanisms: The chapter unravelled the intricacies of addiction in the digital age, transcending traditional boundaries, encompassing behavioural, psychological, and neurological facets to unveil the complexities of technology dependency.

2. Integration of Psychological and Neurological Aspects: It delved into the intersection of psychology and neuroscience, shedding light on how technology triggers the brain's reward system, fostering compulsive behaviours—a critical understanding in deciphering the roots of technology addiction.

3. Spectrum of Addiction Manifestations: Acknowledging the spectrum of addiction, from mild obsession to severe dependency, underscored the multifaceted nature of addictive behaviours, highlighting diverse manifestations across individuals and the potential escalation if left unchecked.

4. Social, Cultural, and behavioural Influences: The exploration extended beyond individual realms, unveiling societal norms, cultural trends, and behavioural psychology as influential factors shaping the acceptance and normalization of excessive technology use—a crucial consideration in the battle against addiction.

5. Impact on Mental Health and Well-being: The chapter elucidated the profound impact of technology addiction on mental health—illuminating anxiety, depression, social withdrawal, and other psychological consequences stemming from excessive digital engagement.

6. Foundation for Effective Intervention and Management: This comprehensive understanding serves as the bedrock—a foundation upon which effective intervention strategies and management approaches can be constructed, aimed at fostering mindful and balanced technology engagement.

7. Importance of Awareness and Proactive Measures: The chapter emphasizes the urgency of awareness and proactive measures, advocating for informed discussions, interventions, and support structures to navigate the complexities of technology addiction.

II.

Impact of Technology Addiction

Chapter 3:

Psychological Effects of Excessive Screen Time

1. Introduction: Unveiling the Psychological Impact of Prolonged Screen Time

Step into a realm where pixels dance on screens, shaping not just visuals but the very fabric of our minds. This chapter serves as a gateway—a passage into the labyrinth of psychological ramifications cast by the prolonged gaze into digital realms. It unfolds the narrative of how excessive screen time etches profound imprints on mental health and well-being, paving the way for a comprehensive exploration of the psychological effects intertwined with extensive technology use.

The Shifting Landscape of Engagement: Screens, omnipresent in our daily lives, have become windows to a multifaceted digital universe. What once started as a convenience has evolved into an era of unprecedented digital immersion—a landscape where prolonged screen time shapes the contours of our psychological landscapes.

Impact on Mental Equilibrium: The screens, though captivating, cast a shadow—leaving traces of their influence on our mental equilibrium. Prolonged engagement sparks a cascade of psychological effects, weaving a tapestry where anxiety, altered mood states, and disrupted cognitive functions emerge as prominent threads.

Unravelling the Psychological Web: This chapter peers into the intricate web of psychological consequences. It endeavours to dissect how excessive screen time intertwines with cognitive, emotional, and behavioural realms, manifesting in nuanced psychological effects that reverberate through our daily lives.

Setting the Stage for Exploration: As the curtains lift on this exploration, it beckons readers into the depths of the psychological impact—inviting a journey that traverses through realms of altered cognition, emotional turbulence, and behavioural imprints left by prolonged screen engagement.

The Imperative for Understanding: This chapter seeks not just to illuminate the psychological effects but to underscore the significance of understanding these impacts—an awareness that serves as a compass, guiding us towards mindful technology engagement in an era where screens are woven into the very fabric of our existence.

2. Cognitive Impacts: Unveiling the Effects on Mental Processes

Step into the realm where cognition intertwines with screens—an intricate tapestry where excessive engagement casts a shadow on cognitive faculties. This section navigates through the cognitive impacts, unveiling the repercussions of prolonged screen time on attention, concentration, multitasking abilities, memory, and learning capabilities.

Attention Deficits and Fragmented Focus: Prolonged exposure to screens fragments attention spans. The constant influx of information, notifications, and stimuli nurtures a distracted mind—diminishing the ability to sustain focus, leading to increased distractibility and reduced attentional capacities.

Decreased Concentration and Cognitive Load: Screens, with their incessant demands, impose a burden on cognitive resources. The juggling act of managing multiple tasks in a digital milieu overwhelms cognitive capacities, resulting in decreased concentration levels and diminished cognitive load management.

Multitasking Challenges in Digital Realms: The allure of multitasking within digital landscapes harbors challenges. Engaging in multiple tasks simultaneously on screens, once hailed as efficiency, splinters cognitive processes, leading to decreased efficiency, errors, and reduced task performance.

Impact on Memory and Learning Abilities: Screens, while repositories of vast information, paradoxically impair memory and learning. The constant exposure to fragmented information impedes deep processing—hindering the encoding and retrieval of information essential for long-term memory consolidation and effective learning.

Adaptation and Neuroplasticity: The brain, an adaptive entity, undergoes neuroplastic changes in response to prolonged screen engagement. This adaptation remodels neural networks—altering cognitive processes and potentially reshaping learning patterns, albeit in ways that might hinder traditional learning mechanisms.

Striving for Cognitive Balance: Understanding these cognitive impacts underscores the importance of striving for cognitive balance amidst the digital deluge. It calls for mindfulness in screen engagement, fostering strategies to preserve attention, concentration, and learning abilities in an era abundant with digital distractions.

3. Emotional Well-being

Examining the emotional aspects, this part discusses the link between excessive screen time and emotional regulation, stress, anxiety, and mood disorders. It explores how constant digital engagement can affect one's emotional state.

3.1. Emotional Well-being: Unraveling the Impact on Emotional States

Step into the emotional realm where screens intertwine with feelings—an intricate web where excessive digital immersion casts ripples on emotional well-being. This section navigates through the emotional impacts, elucidating the intricate connection between excessive screen time and emotional regulation, stress, anxiety, and mood disorders.

Emotional Regulation in Digital Realms: Screens, while captivating, disrupt emotional regulation. The constant stream of digital content, often evoking instant emotional responses, challenges the ability to regulate emotions effectively, leading to emotional volatility and fluctuations in mood states.

Stress Amplification and Anxiety Provocation: Prolonged digital engagement fosters stress amplification. The omnipresent connectivity, notifications, and the fear of missing out (FOMO) contribute to heightened stress levels, fostering anxiety and an overwhelmed emotional state.

Impact on Mood Disorders and Mental Health: Screens cast shadows on mental health, weaving a narrative of mood disorders. Excessive engagement correlates with increased instances of depression, exacerbating existing mood disorders, and serving as a catalyst for emotional turmoil.

Interplay with Social Comparisons and Self-Esteem: Digital realms serve as platforms for social comparisons, impacting self-esteem and emotional well-being. Constant exposure to curated digital lives fosters feelings of inadequacy, triggering emotional distress and altering self-perception.

Disconnection from Real-life Emotions: The allure of screens often disconnects individuals from real-life emotions. Overreliance on digital escapism fosters emotional disconnection, hindering the ability to empathize and engage authentically in offline emotional experiences.

Striving for Emotional Equilibrium: Recognizing these emotional impacts underscores the significance of striving for emotional equilibrium in digital engagements. It calls for conscious efforts to cultivate emotional resilience, disconnect from digital stressors, and foster healthy emotional regulation amidst digital immersion.

4. Sleep Disruptions: Unveiling the Impact on Restful Slumber

Enter the realm where screens blur the boundaries between day and night—a realm where excessive digital engagement disrupts the tranquility of sleep. This segment delves into the intricacies of disrupted sleep patterns, exploring the effects on sleep quality, circadian rhythms, and the prevalence of sleep disorders amid high digital exposure.

Impact on Sleep Quality: Prolonged screen time casts shadows on the realm of restful slumber. Exposure to screens, especially in the evening, suppresses the production of melatonin—the sleep-inducing hormone—impairing sleep quality and delaying the onset of restorative sleep.

Disturbance of Circadian Rhythms: Screens wield the power to disrupt the body's internal clock—circadian rhythms. The blue light emitted by screens interferes with the natural circadian rhythm, prolonging the time taken to fall asleep and affecting the depth and quality of sleep experienced throughout the night.

Prevalence of Sleep Disorders: The prevalence of sleep disorders burgeons in the wake of high digital exposure. Individuals immersed in prolonged screen time often report increased instances of insomnia, delayed sleep phase syndrome, or other sleep disturbances, impacting overall sleep hygiene.

Digital Engagement and Sleep Hygiene: Excessive screen time infiltrates sleep hygiene—an essential component of healthy sleep patterns. The digital allure fosters late-night engagement, compromising the essential practices conducive to sound sleep, such as establishing a relaxing bedtime routine and disconnecting from screens before sleep.

Striving for Sleep Restoration: Understanding these disruptions underscores the importance of striving for sleep restoration amidst the digital landscape. It advocates for digital mindfulness—implementing screen curfews, adopting sleep-friendly habits, and fostering environments conducive to restful slumber.

5. Behavioral Changes: Unveiling Shifts in Actions and Reactions

Enter the realm where screens shape behaviors—a domain where excessive digital immersion orchestrates alterations in social behaviors, decision-making, impulsivity, and the emergence of addiction-like patterns. This section navigates through the behavioral changes intertwined with extended screen time.

Alterations in Social Behaviors: Prolonged digital engagement reshapes the dynamics of social interactions. Individuals engrossed in screens exhibit altered communication patterns, opting for digital interactions over face-to-face engagements, leading to decreased social connectivity and a decline in offline social interactions.

Increased Impulsivity and Instant Gratification: Screens cultivate a culture of instant gratification. The rapid access to information, entertainment, and social validation fuels impulsivity, fostering a need for immediate rewards and diminishing patience in offline endeavors.

Changes in Decision-Making Patterns: Excessive screen time molds decision-making patterns. The constant exposure to online content, often curated to evoke immediate reactions, influences decision-making, impacting the depth and thoughtfulness of offline choices.

Potential for Addiction-like Behaviors: Screens pave the way for addiction-like patterns. Compulsive engagement, the inability to disconnect, and an incessant craving for digital stimuli echo the hallmarks of addictive behaviors, nurturing an environment prone to digital dependencies.

Striking a Balance in Behavioral Patterns: Understanding these behavioral changes accentuates the need for striking a balance. It calls for conscious efforts to recalibrate social interactions, regain patience, restore thoughtful decision-making, and recognize and mitigate addictive tendencies entrenched in digital engagements.

6. Developmental Impacts on Children and Adolescents: Unveiling Effects on Growth and Maturation

Step into the realm where screens shape the formative years—a terrain where excessive digital immersion casts ripples on the development of children and adolescents. This section delves into the multifaceted impacts of screen time on social skills, cognitive development, and emotional regulation among younger populations.

Impact on Social Skills: Prolonged screen time influences the acquisition of social skills. Excessive engagement often replaces real-life interactions, hindering the development of crucial social cues, empathy, and effective communication skills among children and adolescents.

Cognitive Development and Learning Abilities: Screens carve pathways in cognitive development. Excessive exposure can hinder the development of critical thinking, problem-solving abilities, and creativity, potentially impeding academic performance and learning potential in younger individuals.

Emotional Regulation and Well-being: The digital world leaves imprints on emotional regulation. Excessive screen time affects emotional resilience and regulation among children and adolescents, potentially impacting their emotional well-being and mental health during critical developmental stages.

Adverse Effects on Physical Health: Prolonged engagement with screens often correlates with sedentary behaviors, impacting physical health. Reduced outdoor activities, exercise, and playtime can contribute to health concerns like obesity and inadequate physical development among younger populations.

Parental and Educational Guidance: Understanding these developmental impacts emphasizes the role of parental guidance and educational strategies. It calls for informed practices—setting screen time limits, fostering balanced engagement, and promoting offline activities essential for holistic growth and development.

7. Virtual Reality and Mental Health: Navigating Immersive Experiences

Enter the realm where reality blurs, where immersive technologies like virtual reality (VR) carve pathways into new experiences. This section navigates the psychological implications of immersive experiences, distinguishing between recreational use and potential addictive behaviors, and unraveling their impact on mental health.

The Allure of Immersive Realms: Virtual reality, with its captivating immersive experiences, transcends traditional boundaries, offering a gateway to alternate realities. Its allure lies in the ability to transport individuals into fantastical realms, blurring the lines between the physical and digital worlds.

Psychological Implications of Immersive Experiences: VR's immersive nature holds vast psychological implications. While recreational use may enhance entertainment, education, or therapeutic interventions, prolonged and compulsive engagement could potentially lead to addictive behaviors, impacting mental health.

Balancing Recreational Use and Addiction-like Patterns: Distinguishing between recreational use and addictive behaviors becomes pivotal. While controlled engagement in immersive experiences may offer benefits, addictive tendencies linked to compulsive VR usage might disrupt daily functioning, social interactions, and emotional well-being.

Potential Mental Health Impacts: Immersive technologies, when used excessively or compulsively, may intertwine with mental health. Potential consequences might include increased stress, anxiety, dissociation from reality, and a blurring of boundaries between the virtual and real world—impacting emotional and psychological well-being.

Guidelines for Balanced Engagement: Understanding the delicate balance between recreational use and potential addiction-like patterns underscores the importance of guidelines and mindful engagement. It calls for informed practices—setting limits, fostering awareness, and recognizing signs of excessive engagement to preserve mental health amidst immersive experiences.

8. Self-Esteem and Body Image: Unveiling the Influence of Digital Realms

Enter the realm where pixels sculpt perceptions, where social media and digital platforms cast shadows on self-esteem and body image. This segment delves into the pervasive influence of curated content, elucidating its impact on self-perception and contributing to negative body image issues.

Curated Realities in Digital Spaces: Social media platforms offer curated glimpses into lives, showcasing idealized images and lifestyles. These representations often set unattainable standards, fostering comparison and evoking feelings of inadequacy in viewers.

Impact on Self-Esteem: Constant exposure to meticulously crafted content can erode self-esteem. Individuals engrossed in digital platforms may perceive themselves as falling short of the idealized standards, fostering feelings of inferiority and diminishing self-worth.

Contributions to Negative Body Image: Digital spaces perpetuate unrealistic beauty ideals, impacting body image. Continuous exposure to filtered and perfected images may lead to body dissatisfaction, fueling negative body image issues among users striving for unattainable physical perfection.

Comparisons and Unhealthy Perceptions: Social media platforms foster comparisons, leading to unhealthy self-perceptions. Endless scrolling through picture-perfect lives amplifies self-criticism, distorting perceptions of reality and contributing to a skewed self-image.

Striving for Authenticity and Positivity: Recognizing the impact of curated content underscores the need for authenticity and positivity in digital spaces. It calls for promoting realistic portrayals, encouraging self-acceptance, and fostering body positivity to counteract the negative effects on self-esteem and body image.

9. Treatment and Intervention Strategies: Navigating Psychological Impacts

This segment delves into preliminary strategies and interventions aimed at mitigating the psychological effects of excessive screen time. While not exhaustive, these initial insights offer potential avenues for therapies and behavioral interventions to address the impacts:

Behavioral Therapy: Cognitive-behavioral interventions focus on recognizing and modifying maladaptive behaviors associated with excessive screen time. This therapy aims to reshape thoughts and behaviors related to digital engagement, promoting healthier usage patterns.

Mindfulness Practices: Encouraging mindfulness techniques can foster awareness and intentional engagement with digital devices. Mindfulness-based interventions aim to cultivate present-moment awareness, reducing impulsive screen use and promoting balanced engagement.

Digital Detox and Time Management: Implementing structured digital detox periods and time management strategies can help regain control over screen time. Interventions focus on setting limits, scheduling designated screen-free periods, and creating healthy routines to restore balance.

Family and Educational Interventions: Engaging families and educational institutions in discussions and interventions is crucial. Collaborative efforts can include establishing guidelines, educating on healthy screen habits, and promoting open dialogues to address the impacts of excessive screen time.

Support Groups and Counseling: Providing support groups or counseling sessions can offer a platform for individuals struggling with the psychological effects of excessive screen time. These forums aim to provide guidance, encouragement, and a supportive environment for managing digital dependency.

Holistic Well-being Approaches: Encouraging holistic well-being practices—such as exercise, outdoor activities, hobbies, and real-life social interactions—can counterbalance the effects of excessive screen time. These interventions promote overall mental and physical health while reducing screen dependency.

10. Key Takeaways: Understanding Psychological Impacts of Prolonged Screen Time

- **Diverse Psychological Effects**: Prolonged screen time spans a spectrum of psychological impacts across various age groups. From altered cognitive functions and emotional well-being to disrupted sleep patterns and social behavior, its influence is multifaceted.

- **Age-agnostic Implications**: The effects of excessive screen time transcend age barriers, impacting children, adolescents, adults, and older populations differently. Understanding these nuances is crucial in addressing age-specific concerns.

- **Mindful Technology Use for Mental Well-being**: The chapter underscores the necessity of mindful technology use to preserve mental well-being. It emphasizes the importance of awareness and conscious engagement to mitigate the adverse psychological effects associated with excessive screen time.

- **Recognition of Varied Impacts**: Addressing the diverse psychological impacts necessitates recognizing alterations in cognitive abilities, emotional regulation, sleep hygiene, social behaviors, self-esteem, and body image issues induced by prolonged screen engagement.

- **Advocacy for Informed Practices**: Advocating for informed practices is pivotal. Setting screen time limits, fostering digital mindfulness, and encouraging balanced engagement are essential steps in preserving mental health amidst the digital landscape.

♦ **Need for Awareness and Education**: Creating awareness about the diverse psychological effects is imperative. Educating individuals, families, and communities about these impacts fosters proactive measures and interventions to mitigate the negative consequences of excessive screen time.

♦ **Pathways to Preserving Mental Well-being**: Recognizing these impacts paves the way for interventions, therapies, and behavioral modifications aimed at restoring a balanced relationship with technology—essential for safeguarding mental well-being in the digital age.

Chapter 4:

Social Ramifications: Isolation vs. Connectivity

1. Introduction: Balancing Connectivity and Isolation in the Digital Age

Step into a world where connectivity transcends boundaries, a realm where screens promise boundless connections yet harbor the shadows of potential isolation. This chapter unravels the dichotomy between the allure of enhanced connectivity through technology and the looming specter of social isolation induced by excessive digital engagement.

The Promise of Connectivity: Technology heralds an era of unprecedented connectivity. Digital platforms and social media offer gateways to instantaneous connections, fostering a global community and transcending geographical barriers. The allure lies in the promise of bridging distances, fostering relationships, and nurturing communities in the digital sphere.

Potential Consequences of Excessive Engagement: Amidst the promises of connectivity, a paradox emerges. Excessive digital immersion may pave the path to unintended consequences—lurking shadows of social isolation. The very tools designed to connect risk foster isolation as they consume excessive time and attention.

Navigating the Dichotomy: The chapter delves into this dichotomy, unveiling the dual faces of technological connectivity. It navigates through the landscapes of enhanced interactions, vibrant communities, and the flip side where excessive engagement breeds isolation, hindering genuine connections and fostering feelings of disconnectedness.

Understanding the Impact: This exploration aims to dissect the impact of excessive digital engagement on social bonds, relationships, and community structures. It seeks to unravel how these technological marvels, while fostering connectivity, can inadvertently create barriers to genuine human interactions, leading to social estrangement.

Preserving Human Connections: It advocates for preserving the essence of human connections amidst the digital tidal wave. It aims to foster awareness and intentional engagement, striking a balance between leveraging technology for connectivity while safeguarding against the potential erosion of genuine human connections.

2. The Illusion of Connectivity: Unveiling Digital Interaction

Step into the realm where screens weave a facade of connections—a realm where digital communication heralds connectivity yet potentially casts shadows on the depth and authenticity of relationships. This section delves into how technology fosters a perceived sense of connectivity while potentially masking genuine social interaction.

Fostering Perceived Connections: Digital platforms promise instantaneous connections. Social media, messaging apps, and virtual interactions offer constant availability, fostering an illusion of being connected. These tools provide the semblance of closeness, instant responses, and an ever-present digital camaraderie.

Surface-level Interaction: The instantaneous nature of digital communication often leads to surface-level interactions. Quick messages, emojis, and brief exchanges, while convenient, may lack the depth and nuance essential for fostering meaningful connections and understanding.

Impact on Relationship Depth: Digital interactions, while fostering connections, may inadvertently impact the depth of relationships. Reduced face-to-face interactions and reliance on digital conversations might hinder the development of emotional depth, empathy, and genuine understanding within relationships.

Perception vs. Reality: The illusion of connectivity through screens often masks the absence of genuine social interaction. While digital platforms facilitate connections, they might lack the emotional depth and intimacy of in-person interactions, potentially diluting the quality of relationships.

Striving for Authentic Engagement: Recognizing this illusion underscores the need for intentional and authentic engagement. It calls for efforts to bridge the gap between perceived connectivity and genuine interaction—fostering meaningful conversations, deeper connections, and nurturing relationships beyond the confines of screens.

3. Social Media and Relationships: Navigating the Digital Influence

Enter the realm where social media intertwines with relationships—a space where digital platforms shape the dynamics of friendships, family ties, and romantic connections. This section delves into the multifaceted influence of social media on diverse relationships, exploring its effects and potential for superficial interactions.

Friendships in the Digital Sphere: Social media platforms redefine friendships, offering constant connectivity. While enhancing accessibility and maintaining connections over distances, these platforms may foster superficial interactions, potentially diluting the depth and intimacy of friendships.

Impact on Family Dynamics: Social media permeates family dynamics, altering communication patterns. While facilitating instant sharing and updates, it may inadvertently lead to a superficial exchange of information, impacting the emotional depth and genuine connection within familial relationships.

Influence on Romantic Relationships: Social media shapes the landscape of romantic connections. While providing avenues for communication and sharing, it may introduce challenges, fostering comparisons, jealousy, and the allure of curated digital personas, potentially impacting the authenticity of romantic bonds.

Superficial Interactions and Perception Management: The curated nature of social media often fosters superficial interactions. Individuals may craft and present idealized versions of their lives, creating an environment where authenticity and genuine connection take a backseat to managing perceptions.

Striving for Authenticity and Meaningful Connections: Recognizing the dual influence of social media underscores the need for fostering authenticity and meaningful connections. It advocates for conscious engagement—nurturing genuine conversations, transparency, and authentic interactions within relationships beyond the digital veneer.

4. **Digital Communication Challenges: Unveiling the Complexities of Online Interaction**

Step into the realm where pixels carry emotions, a space

where digital communication introduces complexities that impact the conveyance and interpretation of emotions. This segment navigates through the nuances of online interactions, addressing challenges that arise due to the absence of non-verbal cues, potentially leading to misunderstandings and conflicts.

Lack of Non-Verbal Cues: Digital communication strips away vital non-verbal cues—facial expressions, tone, and body language. In text-based or even video-based interactions, the absence of these cues hinders the complete transmission and interpretation of emotions.

Emotional Ambiguity and Misinterpretations: The reliance on text or limited visual cues can lead to misunderstandings. The ambiguity inherent in digital communication may result in misinterpretations of tone, intentions, and emotions conveyed, potentially sparking conflicts or strained relationships.

Conveying Complex Emotions: Nuanced emotions often fall prey to digital limitations. Complex emotions, subtleties, or sarcasm might be challenging to convey accurately, leading to misperceptions and misunderstandings among individuals engaged in online conversations.

Overcoming Communication Barriers: The challenges underscore the importance of conscious communication. Acknowledging these limitations prompts the need for clarity, explicitness, and awareness of how messages might be perceived, mitigating the risk of misinterpretations and conflicts.

Seeking Clarity and Understanding: Efforts to overcome these challenges involve seeking clarity in communication. It involves pausing for comprehension, asking for clarification when needed, and being mindful of potential misinterpretations to foster understanding in digital interactions.

5. Technology's Impact on Community Engagement: Navigating Societal Shifts

Enter the realm where screens intersect with local communities—a space where technology's influence shapes the dynamics of community engagement and civic participation. This section delves into the multifaceted effects, including the decline in face-to-face interactions and the broader societal implications.

Shift in Local Community Dynamics: Technology introduces a shift in the landscape of community engagement. While facilitating virtual connections, it inadvertently contributes to a decline in face-to-face interactions within local communities. Physical gatherings, local events, and neighborhood interactions may dwindle as virtual connections take precedence.

Erosion of Face-to-Face Interactions: The allure of digital connectivity may erode traditional face-to-face engagements within communities. Individuals increasingly turn to digital platforms for social interactions, potentially leading to a decline in the depth and frequency of local community engagements.

Impact on Civic Participation: The shift from local to digital interactions may impact civic participation. Reduced face-to-face engagements might lead to a decline in active involvement in local governance, community initiatives, and volunteerism, potentially affecting the vitality of civic life.

Broader Societal Implications: The decline in local community engagements bears broader societal implications. Diminished local interactions might weaken social bonds, hinder community resilience, and impact the sense of belonging, potentially contributing to feelings of disconnectedness within society.

Balancing Virtual and Physical Engagement: Recognizing these shifts advocates for a balance between virtual and physical engagement within communities. It calls for conscious efforts to preserve face-to-face interactions, foster local community connections, and promote active civic participation amidst the digital landscape.

6. Loneliness and Isolation: Unraveling the Impact of Excessive Technology Use

Step into the realm where screens inadvertently cast shadows of loneliness—a space where excessive technology use intertwines with feelings of isolation and disconnectedness, particularly among vulnerable populations. This section delves into the correlation, addressing potential negative outcomes associated with prolonged digital engagement.

Link Between Technology and Emotional Disconnection: Excessive technology use bears a complex relationship with feelings of loneliness and social isolation. For vulnerable populations, including the elderly, adolescents, and individuals facing mental health challenges, prolonged digital immersion may exacerbate feelings of disconnection from genuine human interactions.

Vulnerable Populations at Risk: Among vulnerable groups, excessive technology use can amplify feelings of loneliness and isolation. For the elderly, technology may act as a barrier to traditional forms of social engagement, leading to increased feelings of seclusion. Similarly, among adolescents, excessive screen time might hinder genuine social interactions, leading to feelings of detachment.

Digital Engagement vs. Authentic Connection: The paradox emerges as digital engagement increases while authentic connections decline. The allure of constant virtual connectivity might mask the absence of meaningful relationships, contributing to a sense of disconnectedness and emotional isolation among vulnerable individuals.

Addressing Vulnerabilities in Digital Spaces: Recognizing these vulnerabilities calls for proactive measures. It involves fostering awareness, providing support networks, and creating inclusive digital spaces that encourage genuine connections, especially for vulnerable populations at risk of feeling isolated due to excessive technology use.

Balancing Technology and Human Connection: Striking a balance between technology and authentic human connections becomes pivotal. It involves promoting mindful technology use, encouraging meaningful interactions, and fostering inclusive digital environments that bridge rather than widen the gap between virtual and real-life connections.

7. Youth and Social Development: Navigating the Impact of Digital Connectivity

Enter the realm where screens intertwine with youth's social journey—a space where constant digital connectivity influences social development, shaping the landscape of social skills, empathy, and the ability to form meaningful relationships. This segment delves into the potential impacts on youth due to perpetual digital engagement.

Impact on Social Skills: The allure of digital connectivity may inadvertently affect the acquisition of traditional social skills among youth. Reduced face-to-face interactions and increased reliance on digital platforms might hinder the development of essential social cues, communication, and conflict-resolution skills.

Empathy and Emotional Understanding: Constant digital immersion might impact the cultivation of empathy and emotional understanding among youth. Reduced exposure to nuanced social interactions may limit the development of empathy, potentially hindering the ability to understand and relate to others' emotions effectively.

Formation of Meaningful Relationships: The digital landscape influences the formation of meaningful relationships among youth. While digital platforms offer connectivity, they might foster superficial interactions, potentially hindering the depth and authenticity of relationships formed during critical developmental stages.

Challenges in Relationship-building: The reliance on digital communication may introduce challenges in building genuine connections. The absence of non-verbal cues and limited face-to-face interactions might hinder the ability to establish and nurture meaningful, long-lasting relationships.

Promoting Digital Balance and Social Skills: Recognizing these impacts calls for a balanced approach. It involves encouraging mindful digital engagement while promoting opportunities for face-to-face interactions, fostering the development of social skills, empathy, and the ability to form authentic relationships among youth.

8. Balancing Connectivity and Real-Life Interaction: Nurturing Genuine Connections

Step into the intersection where digital connectivity meets real-life interactions—a space where fostering genuine connections beyond the digital realm becomes paramount. This section offers strategies to strike a balance, encouraging mindful engagement and authentic interactions:

Designate Tech-Free Zones and Times: Create dedicated spaces and times free from digital distractions. Establishing tech-free zones at home or allocating specific hours devoid of screens encourages face-to-face interactions and fosters genuine connections among family members and friends.

Prioritize Face-to-Face Engagement: Actively prioritize face-to-face interactions. Instead of relying solely on digital communication, seek opportunities for in-person meetings, gatherings, and activities that nurture authentic connections and meaningful conversations.

Engage in Shared Activities: Encourage shared activities that facilitate real-life interactions. Participating in hobbies, sports, volunteering, or community events fosters a sense of camaraderie and strengthens connections beyond the confines of digital platforms.

Cultivate Active Listening and Presence: Practice active listening and being present in conversations. Whether in person or through digital mediums, giving undivided attention fosters deeper connections, understanding, and empathy within relationships.

Encourage Meaningful Communication: Promote meaningful conversations that transcend superficial exchanges. Encouraging open dialogues, sharing experiences, and discussing thoughts and emotions nurtures genuine connections and enriches relationships.

Embrace Digital Detox Periods: Implement regular digital detox periods. Designate specific intervals or days where digital engagement is minimized, allowing for a reset and fostering an appreciation for real-life experiences and connections.

Promote Balanced Engagement: Advocate for a balanced approach to technology use. Emphasize the importance of leveraging digital connectivity while valuing and nurturing real-life interactions as essential components of a fulfilling and connected life.

9. Positive Aspects of Connectivity: Leveraging Technology for Connections

Amidst the complexities, technology catalyzes fostering connections and support systems, transcending geographical barriers, and empowering social initiatives. This section celebrates the positive facets of technology in nurturing connections and support networks:

Facilitating Long-Distance Relationships: Technology acts as a bridge for maintaining relationships across vast distances. Video calls, messaging apps, and social media platforms enable individuals to stay connected, fostering intimacy and support in long-distance relationships that might otherwise be challenging to maintain.

Empowering Social Activism: Digital platforms serve as catalysts for social change and activism. They provide spaces for individuals to mobilize, advocate, and raise awareness about social issues, fostering communities passionate about driving positive societal change and making a tangible impact.

Support Groups and Communities: Online platforms offer avenues for support groups and communities. From mental health support networks to hobby-based communities, these digital spaces provide solace, advice, and a sense of belonging to individuals facing various challenges, fostering a supportive environment.

Networking and Professional Connections: Technology facilitates networking and professional connections. Platforms like LinkedIn offer opportunities for career advancement, connecting individuals with mentors, collaborators, and like-minded professionals worldwide, fostering growth and collaboration.

Global Collaboration and Learning: Digital connectivity fosters global collaboration and learning. Online education, collaborative projects, and forums bring together diverse perspectives, fostering knowledge exchange and enhancing learning experiences across borders.

Enhancing Access to Resources: Technology democratizes access to resources. From online libraries to educational materials and healthcare resources, digital platforms bridge gaps, providing access to information and services, particularly in remote or underserved areas.

10. Community Initiatives and Solutions: Nurturing Healthy Digital Habits

Communities are driving forces in promoting healthy digital habits and rebuilding the social fabric. Through collaborative efforts and local initiatives, communities foster a mindful approach to technology use while revitalizing social connections:

Digital Wellness Programs: Community-driven digital wellness programs aim to educate and raise awareness about healthy technology habits. These initiatives provide workshops, seminars, and resources that encourage mindful digital engagement and promote a balanced approach to technology use.

Creating Tech-Free Spaces: Local communities establish designated tech-free spaces, fostering environments for face-to-face interactions and genuine connections. These spaces encourage individuals to engage without digital distractions, revitalizing social interactions within neighborhoods.

Promoting Inclusive Events: Community-driven events and activities are curated to encourage inclusive participation and foster genuine connections among diverse members. By organizing inclusive gatherings, communities nurture social connections and strengthen the local social fabric.

Collaborative Engagement Campaigns: Collaborative engagement campaigns within communities encourage dialogue about the impact of technology on social connections. Through forums, discussions, and community-driven campaigns, these initiatives promote open conversations about fostering meaningful relationships beyond digital interfaces.

Supporting Local Businesses and Activities: Community initiatives focus on supporting local businesses and activities that encourage physical interactions. By promoting local events, markets, and gatherings, communities foster a sense of belonging and camaraderie among residents.

Building Support Networks: Community-driven support networks cater to diverse needs within neighborhoods. These networks offer a platform for sharing experiences, providing advice, and offering support, cultivating a culture of empathy and understanding.

11. Key Takeaways: Balancing Technology for Authentic Connections

- **Positive Connectivity**: Technology serves as a powerful tool, fostering connections across distances and empowering social initiatives, enabling meaningful relationships, and providing platforms for social activism and support groups.

- **Potential Consequences of Isolation**: Excessive reliance on technology might inadvertently lead to feelings of loneliness, social isolation, and disconnectedness, particularly among vulnerable populations. Constant digital immersion could erode traditional social skills and hinder the formation of authentic relationships.

- **Mindful Digital Interaction**: Striking a balance between digital connectivity and genuine social interactions is crucial. While technology facilitates connections, it's essential to recognize its limitations in fostering deep, meaningful relationships and be mindful of the need for authentic engagement beyond the digital realm.

- **Community Initiatives**: Local communities play a pivotal role in promoting healthy digital habits and revitalizing social connections. Through initiatives like digital wellness programs, tech-free spaces, inclusive events, and support networks, communities foster a culture of balanced technology use and genuine social interactions.

- **Nurturing Authentic Connections**: A conscious and balanced approach to technology use involves fostering meaningful face-to-face interactions, prioritizing genuine conversations, and creating spaces that encourage authentic connections, thereby preserving the richness of human relationships.

- **Embracing a Mindful Approach**: Acknowledging both the positive aspects of connectivity and the potential consequences of excessive digital immersion emphasizes the need for a mindful approach to digital interaction. This awareness fosters a deeper appreciation for genuine social connections amidst the digital landscape.

Chapter 5:

Physical Consequences of Technology Overuse

1. Introduction: Unveiling the Physical Ramifications of Technology Overuse

Enter the sphere where screens intersect with our well-being—a space where the ramifications of excessive technology use on physical health take center stage. This chapter embarks on a journey to uncover the physical implications arising from our digital immersion.

In an era where digital connectivity seamlessly integrates into our daily lives, the pervasive nature of technology poses unforeseen challenges to our physical well-being. From prolonged screen time to sedentary behaviours and the impacts of constant connectivity, this chapter navigates the multifaceted landscape of how technology affects our bodies.

The chapter delves into the far-reaching consequences of our digital habits, exploring the potential adverse effects on posture, eyesight, sleep patterns, and overall physical health. It aims to shed light on how our digital interactions might inadvertently impact our bodies, urging a closer examination of the repercussions of our increasingly digitized lifestyles.

As we delve deeper, the chapter unravels the intricate relationship between excessive technology use and its toll on physical health. It seeks to empower readers with insights into potential challenges and encourages a holistic understanding of the implications, advocating for informed and mindful digital engagement to safeguard our physical well-being amidst the digital age.

2. Sedentary Lifestyle and Health Risks: Unveiling the Consequences of Prolonged Screen Time

Dive into the implications where screens dictate motion—a realm where prolonged screen time intertwines with a sedentary lifestyle, unveiling a host of health risks that pose significant concerns. This section unravels the correlation between extended screen use and its toll on physical health:

1. **Obesity and Weight Management**: Excessive screen time often correlates with reduced physical activity. This sedentary behaviour contributes to a higher risk of obesity and weight-related issues among individuals, particularly children, and adolescents, impacting overall health and well-being.

2. **Cardiovascular Complications**: Prolonged sitting and reduced movement associated with increased screen time can elevate the risk of cardiovascular issues. Sedentary behaviours may lead to higher blood pressure, cholesterol levels, and an increased risk of heart disease among both adults and youth.

3. **Musculoskeletal Strain and Postural Problems**: Long periods of screen use often result in poor posture and musculoskeletal strain. Incorrect ergonomics, such as slouching while using devices, may lead to neck pain, backaches, and repetitive strain injuries impacting the spine and joints.

4. **Metabolic and Hormonal Imbalances**: Sedentary lifestyles resulting from excessive screen time can disrupt metabolic and hormonal balances. Reduced

physical activity levels may impact insulin sensitivity, leading to metabolic issues and potentially contributing to conditions like Type 2 diabetes.

5. **Impact on Mental Well-being**: Beyond physical health, sedentary behaviours can also impact mental health. Reduced movement might exacerbate feelings of stress, anxiety, and depression, affecting overall well-being.

6. **Addressing Sedentary Behaviours**: Encouraging breaks from prolonged screen use, incorporating physical activity into daily routines, and practicing mindful tech habits are essential steps to mitigate the adverse effects of a sedentary lifestyle associated with increased screen time.

3. **Screen-related Health Issues: Unveiling the Toll on Physical Well-being**

Enter the realm where screens cast shadows on physical health—a space where prolonged screen exposure brings forth a spectrum of health concerns. This section navigates through screen-induced health issues that warrant attention:

- **Digital Eye Strain**: Prolonged screen use often leads to digital eye strain, causing symptoms like dry eyes, blurred vision, eye fatigue, and discomfort. The extended focus on screens reduces the blink rate, impacting tear production and leading to eye irritation.

- **Headaches and Visual Discomfort**: Intense screen glare and prolonged exposure to bright screens may trigger headaches and visual discomfort. Straining to focus on screens for extended periods might exacerbate these symptoms, impacting productivity and well-being.

- **Sleep Disturbances from Blue Light Exposure**: Exposure to blue light emitted by screens, especially before bedtime, can disrupt the body's natural sleep cycle. Blue light suppresses melatonin production, affecting sleep quality and potentially leading to insomnia or sleep disturbances.

- **Potential Long-term Vision Impact**: While research is ongoing, there are concerns about the long-term impact of excessive screen use on vision. Prolonged exposure to screens, particularly among children and adolescents, raises questions about potential vision-related issues in the future.

- **Mitigating Screen-related Health Concerns**: Implementing strategies such as taking regular breaks, adjusting screen settings for reduced glare, using blue light filters or glasses, and limiting screen time before bedtime are crucial steps to alleviate these screen-induced health issues.

- **Promoting Visual Health**: Educating individuals on the importance of maintaining visual health, encouraging regular eye check-ups, and practicing the 20-20-20 rule (taking a 20-second break to look at something 20 feet away every 20 minutes of screen time) are essential in preserving vision amidst prolonged screen use.

4. Posture and Musculoskeletal Problems: Unravelling the Impact of Prolonged Technology Use

Enter the realm where screens shape posture—a space where extended screen engagement casts shadows on musculoskeletal health. This segment navigates through the implications of excessive screen time on posture and musculoskeletal well-being:

1. **Poor Posture from Prolonged Screen Use**: Hours spent hunched over screens often lead to poor posture. Maintaining fixed positions while using devices, such as leaning forward or slouching, can strain the spine, neck, and shoulders.

2. **Neck Strain and Pain**: Continuous screen use, especially handheld devices, often leads to "text neck," characterized by neck strain and discomfort due to the downward tilt of the head while viewing screens. This strain can cause muscle tension and pain in the neck and upper back.

3. **Back Aches and Spinal Issues**: Prolonged sitting or slouching during screen use can contribute to backaches and spinal issues. It places added pressure on the lower back, potentially leading to discomfort, muscle stiffness, and even exacerbating pre-existing spinal conditions.

4. **Repetitive Strain Injuries**: Performing repetitive motions while using devices, such as typing on keyboards or swiping screens, may lead to repetitive strain injuries. These injuries affect tendons, muscles, and nerves, causing discomfort or pain in the hands, wrists, or arms.

5. **Ergonomics and Posture Improvement**: Adopting proper ergonomic practices, such as maintaining an appropriate screen-to-eye level, using supportive chairs, and taking frequent breaks to stretch, are vital in mitigating posture-related issues induced by excessive screen time.

6. **Promoting Musculoskeletal Health**: Emphasizing the importance of maintaining good posture, practicing proper ergonomics, and incorporating

regular stretching or strengthening exercises into daily routines can aid in preventing musculoskeletal problems caused by prolonged technology use.

5. Effects on Brain Development and Neurological Health: Unveiling Technology's Influence

- Enter the realm where screens intersect with the brain—a space where prolonged screen exposure shapes neurological health and brain development. This segment navigates through the potential implications of excessive screen time on the brain and neurological well-being:

- Impact on Brain Development: Prolonged exposure to screens, especially during critical developmental stages in childhood and adolescence, may impact brain development. Studies suggest potential alterations in brain structure and connectivity due to excessive screen use, prompting ongoing research on its long-term effects.

- Cognitive Functions and Attention: Extended screen time can influence cognitive functions and attention span, particularly among young users. Constant exposure to fast-paced digital stimuli might affect attentional control, concentration, and information processing.

- Effect on Social and Emotional Learning: Excessive screen use, especially among children, could potentially impact social and emotional learning. Reduced face-to-face interactions and overreliance on digital interactions might hinder the development of essential social skills and emotional intelligence.

- Evolution of Understanding: Ongoing research continues to refine our understanding of technology's influence on neurological health. Neuroscientific studies explore the impact of various screen-based activities on brain functions, shedding light on both the potential benefits and concerns.

♦ Mindful Tech Engagement for Neurological Well-being: Encouraging balanced screen time, promoting activities that stimulate diverse areas of the brain (such as reading, creative endeavors, or physical activities), and fostering a mindful approach to digital engagement is crucial for preserving neurological health.

♦ Educational and Supportive Resources: Providing educational resources for parents, educators, and individuals about the potential impact of screen time on brain development fosters informed decisions and promotes a healthier approach to technology use.

6. Sleep Disturbances and Circadian Rhythm Disruption: Unveiling Screen's Impact on Sleep Health

Enter the realm where screens disrupt slumber—a space where screen time before bedtime casts shadows on the body's natural rhythms. This segment navigates through the intricate relationship between screen exposure and sleep disturbances:

♦ **Blue Light and Sleep Quality**: Screens emit blue light, which suppresses the production of melatonin, the hormone responsible for regulating sleep-wake cycles. Exposure to this light, especially before bedtime, disrupts the body's natural cues for sleep, impacting sleep quality and duration.

♦ **Circadian Rhythm Disruption**: Prolonged screen use, particularly in the evening or before bedtime, disrupts the body's circadian rhythm—the internal clock that regulates sleep-wake cycles. This disruption can lead to difficulties falling asleep, staying asleep, or achieving restorative sleep.

- ♦ **Impact on Sleep Duration and Patterns**: Excessive screen time, especially close to bedtime, often leads to shorter sleep durations and irregular sleep patterns. Sleep fragmentation, characterized by frequent awakenings during the night, may occur, affecting overall sleep quality.

- ♦ **Sleep Hygiene and Digital Habits**: Practicing good sleep hygiene, including limiting screen time before bed, establishing a calming pre-sleep routine, and creating a technology-free sleep environment, is crucial in mitigating the impact of screens on sleep.

- ♦ **Mindful Use for Better Sleep**: Encouraging individuals to prioritize sleep and adopt mindful tech habits, such as setting screen time limits, using blue light filters, or implementing a digital curfew before bedtime, can aid in preserving sleep quality and overall health.

- ♦ **Educational Resources and Strategies**: Providing educational resources on the relationship between screen time and sleep disturbances empowers individuals to make informed choices and adopt healthier digital habits for improved sleep health.

7. **Physical Development in Children and Adolescents: Unveiling Screen Time's Impact**

Enter the realm where screens influence growth—a space where prolonged digital immersion shapes physical development in the young. This segment navigates through the effects of excessive screen time on the physical development and well-being of children and adolescents:

- **Impact on Motor Skills**: Excessive screen time may impede the development of fine and gross motor skills among children. Reduced physical activity and increased sedentary behaviors may hinder the refinement of motor skills crucial for coordination, balance, and dexterity.

- **Sedentary Behavior and Physical Activity**: Extended screen use often correlates with reduced physical activity levels among children and adolescents. This sedentary behavior may lead to potential health concerns, including obesity, cardiovascular issues, and muscular development concerns.

- **Potential Long-term Health Outcomes**: Prolonged screen time during childhood and adolescence may have long-term implications for overall health. The lack of physical activity and its impact on growth and development could potentially contribute to health issues later in life.

- **Promoting Balanced Screen Time**: Encouraging a balanced approach to screen time by incorporating physical activities, sports, outdoor play, and diverse recreational pursuits is crucial for supporting healthy physical development among younger demographics.

- **Educational Initiatives and Parental Guidance**: Providing educational initiatives and guidance for parents, educators, and caregivers about the importance of limiting screen time and promoting active play fosters a holistic approach to supporting physical development in children and adolescents.

- **Encouraging Diverse Activities**: Encouraging children and adolescents to engage in a variety of activities beyond screens—such as sports, hobbies, creative endeavors, and outdoor play—nurtures a well-rounded approach to physical development and overall well-being.

8. Digital Addiction and its Impact on Physical Health: Unveiling the Link

Enter the realm where addiction meets screens—a space where prolonged digital engagement shapes physical health concerns. This segment navigates through the intersection of digital addiction and its repercussions on physical well-being:

- **Extended and Uninterrupted Screen Time**: Digital addiction often leads to extended and uninterrupted screen time. Compulsive use of devices, excessive gaming, or obsessive social media scrolling contribute to prolonged periods of sitting and screen exposure.

- **Sedentary Behaviors and Health Risks**: Digital addiction exacerbates sedentary behaviors, significantly impacting physical health. Prolonged sitting associated with addictive screen use increases the risk of obesity, cardiovascular issues, and musculoskeletal problems.

- **Posture-related Complications**: Addiction-driven prolonged screen use often correlates with poor posture. Persistent digital engagement may lead to neck strain, backaches, and repetitive strain injuries due to incorrect ergonomics and sustained positions.

- **Sleep Disruptions and Circadian Rhythm Disturbance**: Digital addiction can intensify sleep disturbances. Compulsive screen use, particularly before bedtime, disrupts the body's natural circadian rhythm, affecting sleep quality and contributing to sleep-related health issues.

- ♦ **Psychosomatic Impacts**: Addiction to technology might exacerbate psychosomatic symptoms. Increased stress, anxiety, and the emotional toll from addictive behaviors can manifest as physical symptoms, further impacting overall well-being.

- ♦ **Mitigating Physical Impact through Behavioral Changes**: Addressing digital addiction involves implementing behavioral changes, such as setting screen time limits, taking regular breaks, and seeking support or professional guidance for managing addictive behaviors.

9. Strategies for Mitigating Physical Effects of Technology Overuse

Enter the realm of proactive adjustments—a space where mindful practices counterbalance the physical toll of technology. This section navigates through actionable strategies to alleviate the physical impact of excessive screen time:

1. **Ergonomic Practices**:

   - **Optimize Workspace**: Arrange your workstation ergonomically. Adjust the chair height, position the monitor at eye level, and maintain proper posture to reduce strain on the neck and back.

   - **Use Ergonomic Accessories**: Consider ergonomic keyboards, mousepads, or chairs designed to support better posture and reduce the risk of repetitive strain injuries.

2. **Take Regular Breaks**:

   - **Follow the 20-20-20 Rule**: Every 20 minutes, take a 20-second break to look at something 20 feet away. This helps relax the eyes and reduce digital eye strain.

- **Movement Breaks**: Incorporate short breaks into screen time. Stand up, stretch, or walk around to counteract the effects of prolonged sitting.

3. **Establish Digital Boundaries**:

- **Set Screen Time Limits**: Implement time restrictions on-screen use, especially before bedtime, to mitigate disruptions to sleep patterns and improve overall sleep quality.

- **Create Tech-Free Zones**: Designate specific areas in your home as tech-free zones, promoting a break from screens and encouraging other activities.

4. **Prioritize Physical Activity**:

- **Incorporate Exercise**: Balance screen time with physical activities. Engage in regular exercise or outdoor activities to counteract sedentary behaviors associated with screen use.

- **Encourage Movement**: Integrate movement into daily routines, such as taking walks, practicing yoga, or participating in sports to promote better overall physical health.

5. **Practice Mindful Screen Use**:

- **Reduce Blue Light Exposure**: Use blue light filters on screens, or consider wearing blue light-blocking glasses to minimize the impact on sleep patterns.

- **Adopt Screen Dimming**: Dim screens during evening hours to signal the body for the onset of sleep.

6. **Seek Professional Guidance:**

   - **Consult Health Professionals**: If experiencing persistent physical discomfort related to screen use, consult healthcare providers or ergonomic specialists for tailored guidance and solutions.

10. Promoting Physical Activity and Well-being Amidst Screen Time

Enter the realm where movement meets screens—a space where balancing digital engagement with physical activity fosters holistic well-being. This section navigates through strategies to promote physical activity alongside screen use for overall health:

1. **Set Activity Goals:**

   - **Establish Daily Exercise Routines**: Set aside dedicated time for physical activities, such as brisk walks, jogging, cycling, or workouts, ensuring a balance between screen time and movement.

2. **Incorporate Active Screen Time:**

   - **Choose Active Entertainment**: Opt for interactive video games that involve movement, dance-based apps, or workout videos that encourage physical activity while engaging with screens.

3. **Family and Social Activities:**

   - **Engage in Group Activities**: Encourage family or friends to join in physical activities, such as hiking, team sports, or outdoor games, fostering a social environment that prioritizes movement over screen time.

4. **Multitasking with Movement**:

   - **Exercise During Screen Time**: Incorporate light exercises, stretches, or simple movements while watching TV or engaging with screens, promoting physical activity even during leisure screen use.

5. **Tech-Assisted Exercise Programs**:

   - **Utilize Fitness Apps or Wearables**: Explore fitness apps or wearable devices that track physical activity levels, set exercise reminders, and offer guided workouts, making it easier to incorporate exercise into daily routines.

6. **Educational Initiatives and Support**:

   - **Promote Awareness**: Educate individuals, especially children and adolescents, about the importance of balancing screen time with physical activity for overall health and well-being.

11. **Key Takeaways: Recogniz.ing and Addressing Physical Health Implications**

    1. **Physical Health Impacts**: Prolonged technology use, characterized by extended screen time and sedentary behaviors, correlates with various physical health concerns such as obesity, musculoskeletal problems, and disrupted sleep patterns.

    2. **Screen Time and Sedentary Risks**: Excessive screen time often leads to prolonged periods of sitting, which increases the risk of obesity,

cardiovascular issues, and posture-related complications, impacting overall physical well-being.

3. **Ergonomic Practices and Behavioral Changes**: Implementing ergonomic practices, taking regular breaks, and adopting lifestyle adjustments are essential strategies to mitigate the physical impact of technology overuse.

4. **Balancing Screen Time with Physical Activity**: Prioritizing physical activity alongside screen use promotes a balanced lifestyle, fostering holistic well-being and countering the adverse effects of excessive screen time on physical health.

5. **Educational Initiatives and Mindful Tech Engagement**: Encouraging awareness about the importance of recognizing and addressing physical health implications associated with excessive technology use is crucial for fostering healthier digital habits.

6. **Strategies for a Healthier Lifestyle**: Incorporating active screen time, setting activity goals, and promoting family and social activities that prioritize movement over excessive screen use are pivotal in mitigating physical health consequences.

7. **Holistic Approach to Technology Use**: The chapter underscores the necessity of a holistic approach that combines mindful tech engagement with regular physical activity to mitigate physical health risks arising from extensive screen time.

III.

Prevention Strategies

Chapter 6:

Recognizing the Signs of Technology Addiction

1. Introduction: Unveiling Signs of Technology Addiction

Enter the realm where screens lead to dependence—a space where understanding the indicators of technology addiction is key. This chapter sets the stage for comprehending and identifying signs and symptoms crucial for effective intervention:

In today's digitally immersive landscape, the allure of technology often transcends mere usage, evolving into a complex relationship where dependency can ensue. The introduction of this chapter shines a light on the concept of technology addiction, emphasizing the significance of recognizing its signs and symptoms as pivotal steps toward effective intervention and mitigation.

The pervasive integration of technology into various facets of life has given rise to behaviors that extend beyond routine usage. Understanding the nuanced signs and symptoms that delineate normal usage from addictive patterns is vital. This chapter seeks to delineate these indicators, offering insights into the multifaceted nature of technology addiction.

By delving into the intricate manifestations of technology addiction, this chapter aims to equip readers with the knowledge to identify, comprehend, and address the signs and symptoms. Recognizing the subtle shifts in behavior, emotions, and habits becomes a compass guiding interventions and fostering healthier digital habits.

2. Defining Technology Addiction: Differentiating Habitual Use and Addiction

Enter the realm where habit diverges into addiction—a space where understanding the nuances is pivotal. This section navigates through the defining characteristics of technology addiction, drawing a line between habitual use and addictive behavior:

1. **Defining Technology Addiction**: Technology addiction refers to a compulsive, excessive, and problematic pattern of engaging with digital devices or platforms, leading to significant impairment in various aspects of life, such as work, relationships, and mental well-being.

2. **Criteria for Identification**:

   - **Loss of Control**: A key indicator involves a loss of control over technology use despite attempts to cut back or stop. Individuals may struggle to limit their screen time or resist the urge to engage, even when aware of its negative consequences.

   - **Preoccupation and Obsession**: Technology addiction often manifests as a preoccupation or obsession with digital engagement, where thoughts, behaviors, and emotions revolve around screen use, leading to neglect of other essential activities.

   - **Negative Impact on Life**: Addiction results in significant negative consequences across various domains, affecting work, academic performance, relationships, mental health, or physical well-being.

3. **Differentiation from Habitual Use:**

   - **Frequency and Duration**: Habitual use typically involves regular but controlled engagement, whereas addiction is characterized by uncontrollable, excessive, and compulsive behaviors, often leading to negative repercussions.

   - **Functional Impairment**: Technology addiction disrupts normal functioning and well-being, significantly impacting daily life, relationships, responsibilities, or mental health, setting it apart from habitual usage patterns.

4. **Psychological Dependence**: Addiction often involves a psychological dependence on technology, where individuals experience cravings, anxiety, or distress when attempting to reduce or cease screen time, indicating a deeper level of dependency.

5. **Persistent Behavior Despite Negative Consequences**: A defining feature of addiction is the persistence of behaviors despite being aware of their negative effects, leading to a cycle of continued problematic engagement.

3. Behavioral Indicators of Technology Addiction: Observable Signs

Enter the realm where behaviors reveal dependencies—a space where observable signs indicate addictive patterns. This section navigates through the behavioral indicators associated with technology addiction, shedding light on observable signs and behaviors:

1. **Excessive Preoccupation with Devices**:

   • **Obsessive Engagement**: Individuals addicted to technology often exhibit an obsessive preoccupation with digital devices or online activities. Their thoughts are persistently fixated on screens, making it challenging to focus on other tasks or conversations.

2. **Increased Secrecy and Deception**:

   • **Secretive Behavior**: Addiction to technology may lead to increased secrecy or deception regarding online activities. Individuals may hide the extent or nature of their digital engagement, keeping passwords secret or creating alternate accounts.

3. **Neglect of Responsibilities**:

   • **Disregard for Obligations**: Technology addiction often results in neglect of responsibilities and obligations. This can include neglecting work or academic commitments, ignoring household chores, or avoiding social interactions due to excessive screen time.

4. **Escalating Time Spent Online**:

   • **Excessive Screen Time**: A prominent sign is a dramatic increase in the time spent online, surpassing what is considered reasonable or healthy. This prolonged engagement can interfere with daily routines, sleep patterns, and personal relationships.

5. **Withdrawal Symptoms**:

- **Irritability and Distress**: When deprived of screen time, individuals with technology addiction may exhibit signs of irritability, distress, or agitation. They might experience withdrawal-like symptoms when attempting to cut back on digital engagement.

6. **Continued Use Despite Negative Consequences**:

- **Inability to Control Use**: Despite recognizing the adverse effects of excessive screen time on various aspects of life, individuals struggling with technology addiction find it challenging to control or curb their digital engagement.

7. **Escaping Reality or Emotional Avoidance**:

- **Using Technology to Escape**: Technology addiction may serve as a means of escapism from reality or emotional challenges. Individuals may excessively engage with screens to avoid dealing with stress, anxiety, or emotional issues.

4. Psychological and Emotional Signs of Technology Addiction: Understanding Emotional Indicators

Enter the realm where emotions intertwine with dependencies—a space where psychological cues unveil addictive patterns. This section navigates through the psychological and emotional signs indicative of technology addiction, shedding light on emotional indicators related to digital use:

1. **Anxiety and Restlessness**:

- **Anxious Reactions**: Individuals

addicted to technology may experience heightened anxiety or restlessness when unable to access their devices or engage online. This unease can stem from the fear of missing out (FOMO) or the need for constant connectivity.

2. **Irritability and Agitation**:

- **Mood Fluctuations**: Addiction to technology can lead to irritability or agitation, especially when interrupted during digital engagement or when attempts are made to limit screen time.

3. **Mood Swings and Emotional Volatility**:

- **Emotional Fluctuations**: Excessive reliance on technology may cause mood swings or emotional volatility. Individuals may exhibit sudden mood changes, swinging between heightened excitement while engaged online to irritability or low mood when offline.

4. **Dependence on Digital Validation**:

- **Validation-seeking Behavior**: Technology addiction often involves a strong dependence on digital validation, where individuals seek constant approval, likes, or positive feedback on social media platforms, affecting their self-worth and emotional stability.

5. **Deteriorating Mental Well-being**:

- **Impact on Mental Health**: Prolonged technology addiction can contribute to deteriorating mental well-being, leading to increased stress, anxiety disorders, depression, or feelings of isolation due to excessive digital engagement.

6. **Dependency as Coping Mechanism**:

   - **Using Screens to Cope**: Individuals may use technology as a coping mechanism to manage stress, emotional challenges, or unpleasant situations, relying heavily on screens for emotional regulation or distraction.

7. **Obsessive Thoughts and Behaviors**:

   - **Obsessive Patterns**: Persistent thoughts about digital engagement and the inability to disengage from screens, even in situations where it is inappropriate or harmful, can signify an obsession related to technology.

5. Physical Manifestations of Technology Addiction: Recognizing Physical Symptoms

Enter the realm where digital dependence translates into physical tolls—a space where physical manifestations offer cues to addictive behaviors. This section navigates through the physical signs and symptoms associated with technology addiction, shedding light on the physical indicators related to excessive digital engagement:

1. **Digital Eye Strain and Visual Discomfort**:

   - **Eye Strain**: Prolonged screen time often leads to digital eye strain, characterized by symptoms like dry eyes, eye fatigue, blurred vision, or discomfort, particularly after extended periods of staring at screens.

2. **Headaches and Physical Discomfort**:

- **Frequent Headaches**: Excessive screen time can trigger headaches or migraines, often attributed to eye strain, prolonged focus on screens, or poor posture during device use.

- **Musculoskeletal Discomfort**: Maintaining static postures while engaging with screens may lead to musculoskeletal discomfort, manifesting as neck pain, backaches, or discomfort in the wrists and hands.

3. **Fatigue and Sleep Disturbances**:

- **Increased Fatigue**: Excessive digital engagement may lead to increased fatigue or tiredness due to disrupted sleep patterns, reduced physical activity, or eye strain-induced exhaustion.

- **Changes in Sleep Patterns**: Technology addiction might disrupt sleep routines, leading to difficulties falling asleep (insomnia), irregular sleep schedules, or disturbances in the sleep-wake cycle due to prolonged screen exposure, especially before bedtime.

4. **Changes in Eating Habits**:

- **Disrupted Eating Patterns**: Technology addiction can contribute to disrupted eating habits, leading to irregular meal timings, mindless snacking while engaged with screens, or fluctuations in appetite due to prolonged digital engagement.

5. **Physical Exhaustion and Reduced Activity**:

- **Lack of Physical Activity**: Excessive screen time often correlates with reduced physical activity levels, resulting in physical exhaustion, decreased energy levels, or a sedentary lifestyle.

6. **Generalized Ailments and Discomfort**:

- **General Ailments**: Individuals struggling with technology addiction might experience generalized discomfort, including overall fatigue, reduced vitality, or a sense of physical malaise associated with prolonged screen use.

6. Social and Interpersonal Implications of Technology Addiction: Unraveling Impact on Relationships and Engagement

Enter the realm where screens alter social landscapes—a space where social implications highlight the impacts of addictive behaviors. This section navigates through the social and interpersonal implications associated with technology addiction, shedding light on the social indicators related to excessive digital engagement:

1. **Disrupted Relationships and Social Withdrawal**:

- **Impact on Relationships**: Technology addiction often leads to strained relationships due to neglect, decreased communication, or preoccupation with screens at the expense of quality time with family, friends, or partners.

- **Social Withdrawal**: Individuals addicted to technology may exhibit withdrawal from face-to-face interactions, preferring digital engagement over real-world social activities, leading to isolation and reduced participation in social events.

2. **Decline in Academic or Professional Performance**:

   - **Reduced Engagement and Focus**: Technology addiction can impact academic or professional performance, leading to decreased concentration, reduced productivity, or poor performance due to distraction or preoccupation with digital devices.

   - **Negative Academic Outcomes**: Excessive screen time might result in declining grades, missed deadlines, or impaired learning due to a lack of focus or the inability to prioritize tasks effectively.

3. **Compromised Communication Skills**:

   - **Impaired Communication**: Prolonged digital engagement might hinder the development of effective communication skills, resulting in difficulties in maintaining meaningful conversations or expressing oneself outside the digital realm.

4. **Dependency on Virtual Interactions**:

   - **Preference for Virtual Engagement**: Individuals addicted to technology may prioritize online interactions over real-world engagements, relying heavily on digital communication for socializing, potentially hindering the development of genuine relationships.

5. **Impact on Social Dynamics**:

   • **Shift in Social Dynamics**: Technology addiction can alter social dynamics, leading to changes in peer relationships, friendships, or family interactions due to the excessive focus on digital engagement, often resulting in interpersonal conflicts or misunderstandings.

7. **Diagnostic Tools and Screening for Technology Addiction: Assessing Severity and Patterns**

Enter the realm where assessments uncover dependencies—a space where diagnostic tools unveil addictive patterns. This section navigates through the diagnostic tools and screening methods employed to assess technology addiction and its severity:

1. **Questionnaires and Self-Assessment Tools**:

   • **Internet Addiction Test (IAT)**: The IAT is a widely used questionnaire assessing an individual's internet use habits, measuring the extent of dependence and its impact on daily life.

   • **Compulsive Internet Use Scale (CIUS)**: CIUS is another tool that gauges problematic internet usage, examining behaviors indicative of compulsive internet use or addiction.

   • **Smartphone Addiction Scale (SAS)**: SAS is designed to assess smartphone dependency and the impact of excessive smartphone usage on various life domains.

2. **Clinical Interviews**:

   • **Structured Interviews**: Mental health

professionals conduct structured interviews, exploring an individual's digital habits, the impact on daily functioning, and the presence of withdrawal symptoms or psychological distress associated with excessive technology use.

3. **Observational Assessments**:

   - **Behavioral Observation**: Clinicians may conduct behavioral observations to assess an individual's engagement with digital devices, screen time patterns, and the extent to which it interferes with daily activities and social interactions.

4. **Functional Impairment Evaluation**:

   - **Functional Assessment**: Professionals evaluate the functional impairment caused by technology addiction, considering its impact on work, academic performance, relationships, and mental health.

5. **Severity Grading Scales**:

   - **Grading Systems**: Some screening methods incorporate severity grading scales to categorize addiction levels, distinguishing between mild, moderate, and severe dependency on technology.

6. **Diagnostic Criteria Informed by Research**:

   - **Adapting Diagnostic Criteria**: Researchers and clinicians continually refine diagnostic criteria based on emerging research, adapting existing criteria like those used for substance use disorders to better fit technology addiction patterns.

7. **Combination of Assessments**:

- **Multifaceted Evaluation**: Comprehensive evaluations often involve a combination of self-reported questionnaires, clinical interviews, and behavioral assessments to capture the multifaceted nature of technology addiction.

8. **Age-Specific Signs and Vulnerabilities in Technology Addiction: Variations Across Age Groups**

Enter the spectrum where age defines dependencies—a space where signs vary and vulnerabilities manifest differently. This section navigates through the age-specific signs and vulnerabilities associated with technology addiction, shedding light on the variations across different age groups:

1. **Children (Up to 12 Years)**:

- **Excessive Screen Time**: Children may exhibit signs of technology addiction through excessive screen time, preferring digital engagement over other activities, or showing distress when restricted from using devices.

- **Poor Academic Performance**: Reduced focus on academic tasks, declining grades, or difficulties in concentrating due to excessive digital engagement are observed signs.

- **Emotional Outbursts**: Emotional distress, irritability, or tantrums when screen time is limited or interrupted can indicate addiction-related issues.

2. **Adolescents (13-18 Years)**:

- **Social Withdrawal**: Adolescents might display signs of technology addiction through withdrawal from face-to-face interactions, preferring virtual communication over real-world engagements.

- **Academic Decline**: Reduced academic performance, decreased interest in extracurricular activities, or procrastination due to excessive screen time are common indicators.

- **Sleep Disturbances**: Changes in sleep patterns, including difficulties falling asleep or disrupted sleep due to late-night screen use, are prevalent signs among adolescents.

3. **Adults (19-65 Years)**:

- **Work Interference**: Technology addiction may impact work productivity, with signs such as decreased efficiency, distraction during work hours, or frequent use of devices at the expense of professional responsibilities.

- **Relationship Strain**: Strained relationships or conflicts arising from neglect of family time, reduced communication, or prioritizing digital engagement over personal relationships can be observed.

- **Mental Health Challenges**: Increased stress, anxiety, or symptoms of depression due to excessive screen time and constant connectivity may be prevalent among adults

4. **Elderly (65+ Years)**:

- **Isolation and Loneliness**: Elderly individuals might exhibit signs of technology addiction through isolation or loneliness, preferring digital interactions over in-person connections.

- **Navigational Challenges**: Difficulty in navigating digital interfaces or becoming easily overwhelmed by technology may be indicators of vulnerability.

- **Health Impact**: Physical strain due to prolonged screen time, coupled with potential challenges in adapting to new technologies, can impact the elderly's health and well-being.

9. Cultural and Contextual Considerations in Technology Addiction: Influence on Recognition and Acceptance

Enter the landscape where cultures shape dependencies—a space where recognition varies and acceptance hinges on societal norms. This section navigates through the cultural and contextual considerations impacting the recognition and acceptance of technology addiction signs:

1. **Cultural Norms and Acceptance**:

- **Varied Perceptions**: Cultural norms influence the perception of technology use. In some cultures, heavy reliance on technology might be accepted as a norm, making it challenging to identify addiction signs due to the widespread acceptance of excessive screen time.

- **Stigma and Denial**: In certain cultural contexts, acknowledging addiction-related behaviors might carry a stigma or be met with denial, hindering the recognition of problematic digital engagement.

2. **Technology in Social Fabric**:

- **Embedded in Daily Life**: Cultures that deeply integrate technology into daily life might find it challenging to distinguish between normal usage and addiction, as technology becomes an inseparable part of societal norms.

- **Community Influence**: Societies where technology use is heavily endorsed or encouraged may overlook addiction signs, considering digital proficiency as a positive trait rather than assessing its potential drawbacks.

3. **Generational and Family Views**:

- **Generational Divide**: Variances in views on technology addiction might exist between generations, with older generations perceiving excessive screen time as problematic while younger generations view it as routine behavior.

- **Family Dynamics**: In family-oriented cultures, technology addiction signs might manifest differently. While some families might recognize and address these signs, others might overlook or normalize them within familial dynamics.

4. **Media and Pop Culture Influences**:

   - **Portrayal of Technology**: Media representations and pop culture influences might shape perceptions of technology use. Positive depictions of constant connectivity could normalize addictive behaviors, impacting the recognition of addiction signs.

5. **Ethnic and Socioeconomic Factors**:

   - **Differential Access and Impact**: Socioeconomic disparities or ethnic differences can influence access to technology and its impact. Recognition of addiction signs might vary based on access levels and the social acceptance of technology within specific demographics.

6. **Cultural Adaptations in Diagnosis**:

   - **Cultural Sensitivity in Diagnosis**: Diagnostic criteria for technology addiction may need cultural adaptations to account for diverse perceptions and norms, ensuring a more comprehensive understanding across cultural contexts.

10. Preventive Measures and Early Intervention for Technology Addiction: Nurturing Healthy Tech Habits

Enter the proactive sphere where habits shape dependencies—a space where prevention and intervention intercede. This section navigates through the preventive measures and early intervention strategies aimed at curtailing technology addiction before escalation:

1. **Education and Awareness Programs**:

   - **Promoting Digital Literacy**: Initiatives focusing on educating individuals about healthy technology use, emphasizing digital literacy, responsible online behavior, and the potential risks of excessive screen time.

   - **Parental and Caregiver Guidance**: Providing guidance to parents and caregivers on setting boundaries, monitoring screen time, and fostering a balanced tech environment for children and adolescents.

2. **Establishing Healthy Tech Habits**:

   - **Setting Screen Time Limits**: Encouraging individuals to set limits on screen time, employing tools like parental controls or apps that monitor usage to promote mindful digital engagement.

   - **Tech-Free Zones**: Designating specific areas or times as tech-free zones within homes, schools, or workplaces to encourage unplugged activities and face-to-face interactions.

3. **Building Resilience and Coping Skills**:

   - **Stress Management Techniques**: Teaching stress reduction techniques, mindfulness practices, and healthy coping mechanisms to manage emotions without solely relying on digital distractions.

   - **Promoting Offline Activities**: Encouraging diverse offline activities such as hobbies, sports, arts, or social gatherings to cultivate well-rounded interests beyond digital engagement.

4. **Creating Supportive Environments**:

   • **Community Support Groups**: Establishing community-based support groups or peer networks for individuals experiencing technology addiction, providing a supportive environment for sharing experiences and seeking help.

   • **School-Based Interventions**: Implementing interventions within educational settings, including workshops, counseling services, or educational modules addressing responsible technology use and mental health.

5. **Professional Counseling and Therapy**:

   • **Early Intervention Programs**: Offering counseling services or therapy sessions specifically tailored to address addictive behaviors related to technology use, intervening at early stages to prevent escalation.

   • **Family Therapy**: Involving family members in therapy sessions to address communication breakdowns or conflicts arising from excessive digital engagement within familial dynamics.

6. **Policy and Regulation**:

   • **Regulatory Measures**: Advocating for policies or guidelines by educational institutions, workplaces, or government bodies to regulate screen time, promote digital wellness, and enforce healthy tech practices.

11. Seeking Professional Help for Technology Addiction: Navigating Mental Health Support

Enter the realm where guidance shapes recoveries—a space where seeking help empowers change. This section navigates through the importance of seeking professional assistance and guidance for individuals dealing with technology addiction:

1. **Recognizing the Need for Support:**

   - **Self-Assessment:** Acknowledging personal struggles and recognizing when digital engagement starts impacting daily life, relationships, or mental well-being, signaling the need for professional assistance.

   - **Family and Friend Support:** Encouraging family members or friends to support and encourage seeking professional help for technology addiction, fostering an environment of understanding and acceptance.

2. **Mental Health Professionals:**

   - **Therapists and Counselors:** Encouraging individuals to seek guidance from licensed therapists, psychologists, or counselors specializing in behavioral addictions or technology-related dependencies.

   - **Specialized Programs:** Exploring programs specifically designed to address technology addiction, ensuring tailored interventions and support.

3. **Support Groups and Communities**:

- **Peer Support Networks**: Engaging with support groups or online communities dedicated to technology addiction recovery, providing a platform for shared experiences, empathy, and guidance.

- **Group Therapy Sessions**: Participating in group therapy sessions led by mental health professionals, fostering camaraderie and mutual support among individuals facing similar challenges.

4. **Clinical Assessment and Treatment**:

- **Comprehensive Assessment**: Undergoing a comprehensive clinical assessment to determine the extent of addiction, underlying factors, and personalized treatment plans tailored to individual needs.

- **Cognitive Behavioral Therapy (CBT)**: Participating in CBT sessions or other evidence-based therapies to address addictive behaviors, reframe thoughts, and develop healthier coping mechanisms.

5. **Family Involvement in Therapy**:

- **Family Therapy Sessions**: Involving family members in therapy sessions to address communication breakdowns or conflicts arising from excessive digital engagement within familial dynamics, fostering understanding and support.

6. **Continued Support and Follow-Up**:

- **Post-Treatment Support**:

Emphasizing the importance of continued support post-treatment, whether through follow-up sessions, support groups, or ongoing counseling to maintain progress and prevent relapse.

12. Key Takeaways: Recognizing Signs and Symptoms of Technology Addiction

1. **Early Recognition for Effective Management:**

   - Identifying signs and symptoms of technology addiction across diverse age groups, contexts, and impacts is crucial for early intervention.

2. **Multi-faceted Signs Across Life Domains:**

   - Technology addiction manifests through behavioral, psychological, physical, and social indicators, impacting various aspects of an individual's life.

3. **Cultural and Contextual Influences:**

   - Acknowledging cultural norms, societal contexts, and generational differences is essential in understanding how technology addiction signs vary across different environments.

4. **Proactive Measures for Prevention:**

   - Implementing preventive measures, promoting healthy tech habits, and intervening early is vital in mitigating the escalation of technology addiction.

5. **Seeking Professional Assistance:**

   - Recognizing the need for professional

help, engaging with mental health professionals, and support groups, and seeking tailored interventions are pivotal steps toward recovery.

6. **Continued Support and Awareness**:

   - Sustaining ongoing support, both post-treatment and within communities, and raising awareness about technology addiction are fundamental in fostering healthy tech use.

7. **Empowering Change Through Recognition**:

   - Acknowledging and understanding signs and symptoms serve as the cornerstone for individuals to take charge of their digital habits and seek the necessary support.

Chapter 7:

Building Healthy Tech Habits for Individuals and Families

1. Introduction: Cultivating Balanced Tech Habits

Welcome to a chapter dedicated to fostering mindful tech habits that harmonize digital engagement with well-being. In an age where technology is omnipresent, striking a balance between its convenience and its impact on our lives becomes paramount.

This chapter embarks on a journey toward cultivating healthy tech habits, recognizing that our relationship with technology profoundly influences our daily routines, relationships, and mental well-being. From individuals navigating personal screens to families negotiating shared digital spaces, the aim is to establish practices that enrich rather than detract from our lives.

By exploring strategies and approaches tailored to individuals and families alike, this chapter seeks to empower readers with the tools necessary to forge a harmonious coexistence with technology. It emphasizes the importance of conscious tech usage, recognizing when, where, and how much technology should play a role in our lives to foster healthier relationships with our devices and each other.

Join us as we delve into actionable insights, practical guidance, and mindful techniques aimed at building a balanced and fulfilling relationship with technology for individuals and families in today's digital landscape.

2. **Understanding Healthy Tech Habits: A Balanced Approach to Digital Consumption**

    1. **Mindful Usage Patterns**:

        • **Purposeful Engagement**: Healthy tech habits entail engaging with digital devices and platforms intentionally, focusing on tasks or activities that align with personal or professional goals.

        • **Conscious Screen Time**: Prioritizing quality over quantity, allocating dedicated and limited time for digital activities while being mindful of potential distractions.

    2. **Digital Boundaries and Balance**:

        • **Establishing Limits**: Setting clear boundaries around tech usage, whether through designated screen-free periods, setting time limits, or establishing tech-free zones within living spaces.

        • **Balancing Offline Activities**: Encouraging a balance between digital engagement and offline pursuits such as hobbies, physical activities, or face-to-face interactions to nurture holistic well-being.

    3. **Tech-Free Zones and Times**:

        • **Designating Tech-Free Spaces**: Allocating areas at home or during family gatherings where digital devices are restricted to promote quality face-to-face interactions and present-moment engagement.

- **Unplugging Routines**: Instituting daily or weekly unplugging rituals, such as device-free meals or family activities, to foster genuine connections and reduce dependency on screens.

4. **Prioritizing Mental Health and Well-being**:

- **Monitoring Emotional Responses**: Being attentive to emotional cues triggered by technology use, taking breaks when feeling overwhelmed, and practicing self-care to maintain emotional balance.

- **Promoting Digital Detox**: Recognizing the value of periodic digital detoxes or breaks to reset and recharge, prioritizing mental health, and reducing reliance on constant digital connectivity.

5. **Healthy Tech Role Models**:

- **Setting Examples**: Modeling healthy tech habits as adults or parents within families, showcasing responsible usage and balanced engagement for younger members to emulate.

- **Open Communication**: Fostering open discussions within families about healthy tech boundaries, ensuring mutual respect and understanding of individual preferences.

6. **Adaptive and Sustainable Practices**:

- **Flexibility and Adaptability**: Embracing flexible tech habits that adapt to changing circumstances or personal needs, ensuring that habits remain sustainable and adaptable over time.

3. **Setting Boundaries and Establishing Tech Rules: Fostering Healthy Digital Environments**

1. **Defining Clear Boundaries**:

   - **Designated Tech-Free Zones**: Allocating specific areas within homes or shared spaces where digital devices are prohibited, fostering unplugged interactions and minimizing distractions.

   - **Scheduled Tech-Free Times**: Designating specific times during the day or week for tech-free activities or family bonding, promoting face-to-face engagement and genuine connections.

2. **Family Agreements and Tech Guidelines**:

   - **Collaborative Discussions**: Engaging family members in open discussions to co-create guidelines or agreements regarding acceptable tech usage, fostering a shared understanding and respect for each other's preferences.

   - **Establishing Mutual Rules**: Setting rules that cater to the family's dynamics, considering factors like age, and individual needs, and ensuring the guidelines are agreed upon by all members.

3. **Consistent Reinforcement**:

   - **Clear and Consistent Communication**: Communicating and reinforcing established tech rules consistently, ensuring adherence to boundaries, and addressing deviations with understanding and reinforcement.

- **Lead by Example**: Adults setting a positive example by adhering to the agreed-upon tech rules, showcasing responsible and balanced tech habits for younger family members to emulate.

4. **Tech-Free Rituals and Activities**:

- **Family Tech-Free Time**: Implementing regular activities or rituals, like tech-free dinners, game nights, or outdoor excursions, encouraging quality family time devoid of digital distractions.

- **Designated Screen Time Limits**: Establishing clear time limits for individual screen time, promoting self-regulation and balanced usage among family members.

5. **Adaptable Guidelines**:

- **Flexibility and Adaptability**: Creating guidelines that remain adaptable to accommodate occasional exceptions or changing circumstances while ensuring the primary focus remains on promoting healthy tech habits.

6. **Open Dialogue and Evaluation**:

- **Regular Review and Discussions**: Conduct periodic reviews of established tech rules, encouraging open dialogues within the family to address any evolving concerns or necessary modifications.

4. **Modeling Healthy Behavior: Leading by Example in Tech Use**

   1. **Parental Influence and Modeling**:

      - **Setting the Tone**: Parents serve as primary role models in shaping children's attitudes and behaviors towards technology. Demonstrating responsible and balanced tech usage sets a strong foundation.

      - **Consistent Behavior**: Consistency in practicing healthy tech habits reinforces their importance and provides a clear example for children to emulate.

   2. **Mindful Tech Engagement**:

      - **Intentional Device Usage**: Demonstrating purposeful tech use by prioritizing meaningful activities over mindless scrolling or excessive screen time, showcasing the value of moderation.

      - **Respecting Tech Boundaries**: Adhering to established tech-free times or zones within the household, illustrating the significance of balanced engagement and respecting boundaries.

   3. **Open Communication and Involvement**:

      - **Transparent Discussions**: Engaging in open discussions with children about personal tech habits, explaining the reasons behind established rules, and seeking their input fosters mutual understanding.

      - **Active Participation**: Actively participating in tech-free family activities or bonding moments, emphasizing the importance of present-moment engagement and genuine connections.

4. **Consistency in Rule Adherence**:

    • **Upholding Family Agreements**: Demonstrating consistency in adhering to established tech guidelines ensures that children witness the application of mutually agreed-upon rules consistently.

    • **Positive Reinforcement**: Providing positive reinforcement or acknowledging adherence to tech rules encourages children to follow suit and reinforces the importance of responsible tech usage.

5. **Creating Shared Experiences**:

    • **Shared Offline Activities**: Initiating and actively engaging in non-tech-related family activities or hobbies promotes bonding and demonstrates the value of diverse, offline experiences.

6. **Parental Self-Reflection and Adaptability**:

    • **Self-Reflection**: Parents periodically reflect on their tech habits and adapt them if necessary, demonstrating a growth mindset and willingness to change for the better.

    • **Adapting to Individual Needs**: Understanding that tech habits may vary among family members and adapting parenting approaches to cater to individual needs and ages.

5. **Promoting Digital Literacy and Responsibility**

5.1. Promoting Digital Literacy and Responsibility: Educating for Safe and Informed Tech Use

1. Teaching Digital Literacy:

- **Understanding Online Platforms**: Educating children about various online platforms, their functionalities, and the potential risks associated with them.

- **Navigating Online Information**: Teaching critical evaluation skills to discern credible sources from misinformation or unreliable content, fostering a healthy skepticism towards online information.

2. Responsible Online Behavior:

- **Online Etiquette and Safety**: Instilling values of respect, kindness, and digital etiquette, emphasizing the importance of cyber safety, privacy settings, and avoiding sharing personal information online.

- **Addressing Cyberbullying**: Educating on recognizing and responding to cyberbullying, encouraging open communication about online experiences, and seeking help if faced with such situations.

3. Understanding Digital Footprints:

- **Awareness of Online Presence**: Teaching about the concept of digital footprints and the potential long-term implications of online actions or posts, promoting responsible online behavior from an early age.

- **Importance of Privacy Settings**: Empowering children to manage privacy settings on social platforms and understand the impact of sharing content online.

4. **Critical Thinking Skills**:

- **Evaluating Online Content**: Cultivating critical thinking skills to analyze and question online content, encouraging children to approach online information with discernment and skepticism.

- **Identifying Manipulative Content**: Teaching strategies to recognize and respond to manipulative content, including clickbait, fake news, or misleading advertisements.

5. **Engaging Parental Guidance**:

- **Open Communication**: Encouraging open dialogue between parents and children about online experiences, fostering an environment where children feel comfortable seeking guidance or discussing online concerns.

- **Supervised Online Activities**: Gradually introducing age-appropriate online activities under parental guidance to teach responsible tech usage and safety practices.

6. **Collaborative Learning and Support**:

- **School and Community Involvement**: Collaborating with schools and community programs to integrate digital literacy and responsible tech use into educational curricula, creating a cohesive learning environment.

6. Encouraging Mindful Tech Use: Cultivating Awareness in Digital Engagement

1. Tech Usage Awareness:

- **Purposeful Engagement**: Encouraging individuals to pause and reflect on the purpose behind using technology, fostering intentionality in each digital interaction.

- **Checking Intentions**: Prompting users to ask themselves why they're using a specific app or device, ensuring alignment with their goals or values.

2. Mindful Consumption Practices:

- **Breath Awareness**: Incorporating mindful breathing exercises or short pauses before and during tech usage to center attention and maintain present-moment awareness.

- **Sensory Awareness**: Encouraging users to notice sensory experiences while using technology, such as touch, sight, or sound, fostering a deeper connection with the present moment.

3. Establishing Tech-Free Moments:

- **Mindful Breaks**: Encouraging periodic breaks during tech usage to refocus attention, relax the mind, and avoid prolonged screen exposure.

- **Setting Tech Boundaries**: Scheduling specific periods for tech-free activities or implementing digital detox days to foster a healthier tech-life balance.

4. **Conscious Digital Engagement**:

   - **Focused Attention**: Advising individuals to engage in one task at a time, avoiding multitasking, and dedicating full attention to the present activity or conversation.

   - **Noticing Tech Impact**: Prompting reflection on the emotional or mental state before and after tech usage, recognizing the impact on mood or focus.

5. **Mindful Tech Rituals**:

   - **Tech Mindfulness Reminders**: Utilizing tech itself as a reminder for mindfulness practices, such as setting mindful app notifications or using apps that encourage breaks or mindful moments.

   - **Gratitude for Tech Use**: Cultivating gratitude for the beneficial aspects of technology while being mindful of its limitations or potential negative impacts.

6. **Mindful Parenting Approaches**:

   - **Parental Guidance**: Encouraging parents to model and teach mindful tech practices to children, fostering an environment where balanced and conscious tech use is embraced.

7. **Community Support and Mindfulness Programs**:

- **Group Practices**: Encouraging community-based mindfulness activities or programs focused on tech usage awareness, providing support and reinforcement for mindful tech habits.

7. **Utilizing Technology for Positive Purposes: Balancing Functionality and Recreation**

1. **Educational Platforms and Learning Tools**:

- **Online Learning Resources**: Promoting the use of educational apps, platforms, and online courses that supplement traditional learning, offering diverse and engaging ways to acquire knowledge.

- **Skill Development**: Encouraging the use of technology for skill-building through tutorials, language-learning apps, coding platforms, or creative software.

2. **Creative Expression and Innovation**:

- **Artistic Endeavors**: Encouraging creative pursuits through digital art, music composition software, video editing tools, or writing applications, fostering avenues for self-expression and creativity.

- **Innovative Projects**: Highlighting the potential for innovation and problem-solving by engaging with technology for research, STEM projects, or entrepreneurial endeavors.

3. **Professional Development and Productivity**:

   - **Remote Work Tools**: Emphasizing the benefits of technology for remote work, utilizing communication platforms, project management tools, and collaborative software to enhance productivity.

   - **Time Management Apps**: Encouraging the use of technology for time-tracking, task management, and organizational tools to optimize efficiency in both personal and professional domains.

4. **Health and Wellness Applications**:

   - **Fitness and Well-being**: Advocating the use of health-tracking apps, meditation or mindfulness platforms, and nutritional resources to support physical and mental well-being.

   - **Telemedicine Services**: Highlighting the accessibility and benefits of telehealth services, providing medical consultations and mental health support via technology.

5. **Community Engagement and Activism**:

   - **Social Causes**: Encouraging participation in online activism, fundraising campaigns, or community projects facilitated through technology, fostering engagement in social causes.

6. **Balancing Functional and Recreational Use**:

   - **Mindful Recreational Use**:

Promoting the balance between utilizing technology for productive, functional purposes and allocating leisure time for recreational tech use to unwind or entertain responsibly.

- **Setting Priorities**: Encouraging individuals to prioritize and allocate time effectively, ensuring that recreational tech use doesn't overshadow functional or productive endeavors.

8. **Engaging in Offline Activities: Embracing Non-Digital Pursuits**

    1. **Exploring Hobbies and Interests**:

        - **Outdoor Pursuits**: Encouraging activities like hiking, gardening, or sports that allow individuals to connect with nature and engage in physical exercise.

        - **Creative Endeavors**: Promoting hobbies such as painting, crafting, playing musical instruments, or cooking that foster creativity and offer a break from digital screens.

    2. **Social and Interpersonal Engagement**:

        - **Face-to-Face Interactions**: Advocating for in-person gatherings, socializing with family and friends, and fostering meaningful connections beyond digital communication.

        - **Group Activities**: Encouraging participation in group activities like book clubs, volunteering, or community events that promote social bonding and engagement.

3. **Mindfulness and Relaxation Practices**:

   - **Mindfulness and Meditation**: Introducing mindfulness practices, yoga, or relaxation techniques that provide moments of calm and rejuvenation away from screens.

   - **Reading and Unplugging**: Promoting reading physical books or engaging in activities that involve unplugging from technology, allowing for mental relaxation.

4. **Physical Exercise and Wellness**:

   - **Fitness Routines**: Encouraging regular physical exercise, whether through gym workouts, outdoor runs, or home workout routines, promoting overall health and well-being.

   - **Nature Walks or Outdoor Activities**: Advocating for time spent outdoors, whether walking in parks, visiting natural landscapes, or engaging in outdoor recreational activities.

5. **Cultivating Personal Relationships**:

   - **Quality Time with Loved Ones**: Emphasizing the importance of spending quality time with family and friends through meaningful conversations, shared experiences, and bonding activities.

   - **Creating Tech-Free Zones**: Designating specific areas or times in the household where digital devices are minimized to encourage offline interactions.

6. **Balancing Digital and Offline Activities**:

- **Setting Limits**: Encouraging individuals to set specific time limits for screen use and allocate dedicated periods for offline pursuits to maintain a healthy balance.

- **Prioritizing Offline Time**: Advocating for the prioritization of offline activities and experiences that enrich life beyond the digital sphere.

9. Fostering Communication and Connection: Nurturing Open Dialogue on Technology Use

1. **Family Tech Talks**:

- **Scheduled Discussions**: Encouraging regular family meetings or dedicated sessions to openly discuss technology use, allowing everyone to share their experiences, concerns, and preferences.

- **Creating a Safe Space**: Fostering an environment where family members feel comfortable expressing their thoughts and concerns about technology without judgment.

2. **Active Listening and Empathy**:

- **Understanding Perspectives**: Encouraging active listening among family members to understand each other's viewpoints regarding technology preferences, challenges, and boundaries.

- **Empathetic Discussions**: Cultivating empathy towards varying needs or concerns related to technology use within the family dynamic.

3. **Setting Family Guidelines**:

- **Collaborative Rule-setting**: Involving all family members in establishing guidelines or agreements about tech usage, considering individual needs, and collectively setting boundaries for screen time or device usage.

- **Consistency and Flexibility**: Striking a balance between consistent rules and flexibility, allowing for adjustments based on changing circumstances or specific situations.

4. **Tech-Free Quality Time**:

- **Designated Tech-Free Zones**: Establishing areas or times within the household for tech-free interactions, fostering undistracted family bonding moments.

- **Engaging Activities**: Planning and engaging in activities that encourage interaction without screens, such as board games, outdoor outings, or shared hobbies.

5. **Encouraging Openness and Support**:

- **Supportive Environment**: Creating a supportive atmosphere where family members can openly seek help or advice if they encounter challenges related to technology use.

- **Respect for Individual Preferences**: Acknowledging and respecting individual differences in tech preferences and usage habits within the family.

6. **Continuous Check-ins**:

- **Periodic Reviews**: Scheduling periodic check-ins to assess how the agreed-upon tech guidelines are working for everyone, allowing for adjustments or modifications if necessary.

- **Celebrating Positive Changes**: Recognizing and celebrating positive changes or efforts made in aligning with the agreed-upon tech habits and guidelines.

10. **Adapting Habits as Technology Evolves: Embracing Continuous Assessment and Adjustment**

1. **Technology Assessment**:

- **Periodic Evaluation**: Encouraging regular assessments of new technologies or changes in digital trends within the household, considering their impact on habits and routines.

- **Staying Informed**: Staying updated on advancements and potential risks associated with emerging technologies, allowing for informed decision-making.

2. **Flexible Guidelines**:

- **Dynamic Rule Adaptation**: Promoting flexible guidelines that can evolve with technological advancements, ensuring that established rules remain relevant and effective.

- **Discussion-based Updates**: Facilitating family discussions on potential adjustments in tech habits or rules, considering the impact of new devices or apps on daily life.

3. **Educational Approaches**:

- **Tech Literacy**: Emphasizing the importance of ongoing education and discussions about responsible and safe technology use, especially with new or unfamiliar devices or applications.

- **Learning Together**: Engaging in learning experiences as a family to understand and explore new tech features or functionalities, fostering shared knowledge and understanding.

4. **Risk Assessment and Mitigation**:

- **Anticipating Risks**: Discussing potential risks or drawbacks associated with new technologies, and exploring ways to mitigate negative impacts on well-being or relationships.

- **Establishing Protocols**: Creating protocols or guidelines to address concerns or risks related to emerging tech, ensuring proactive measures are in place.

5. **Trial Periods and Reflection**:

- **Trial Runs**: Allowing for trial periods with new technologies before integrating them fully into daily routines, assessing their impact on family dynamics and individual habits.

- **Reflective Discussions**: Holding reflective discussions post-trial to evaluate the benefits and drawbacks of new tech implementations, considering adjustments based on experiences.

6. **Encouraging Adaptability**:

   - **Open-mindedness**: Fostering an open-minded approach towards change and adaptation, recognizing that habits and rules may need revision to suit evolving technological landscapes.

   - **Shared Decision-making**: Involving all family members in discussions and decision-making processes regarding adaptations, encouraging a sense of ownership in tech-related changes.

11. Community Support and Resources: Accessing Assistance for Healthy Tech Habits

1. **Support Groups and Workshops**:

   - **Local Support Networks**: Highlighting local community groups, organizations, or clubs that focus on digital wellness, providing opportunities for in-person meetings, discussions, and shared experiences.

   - **Workshops and Seminars**: Promoting workshops or seminars conducted by professionals or experts in the field, offering guidance on fostering healthy tech habits.

2. **Online Forums and Platforms**:

   - **Virtual Communities**: Encouraging participation in online forums, social media groups, or dedicated platforms focusing on digital well-being, allowing individuals to seek advice, share experiences, and access resources from diverse perspectives.

- **Educational Websites and Blogs**: Recommending reputable websites, blogs, or online resources dedicated to digital wellness, offering tips, articles, and tools for managing tech usage.

3. **Professional Services and Counseling**:

- **Therapeutic Support**: Highlighting the availability of mental health professionals specializing in technology addiction or digital wellness, offering counseling, therapy, or consultations for individuals or families.

- **Family Counseling Services**: Identifying family counseling services that specifically address tech-related issues, providing a structured approach to managing tech habits collectively.

4. **Community Events and Campaigns**:

- **Awareness Campaigns**: Promoting local or national campaigns focused on digital wellness, raising awareness about healthy tech habits, and providing resources for individuals and families.

- **Community Events**: Encouraging participation in community events or initiatives centered around mindfulness, tech-free days, or family activities that foster healthy relationships beyond technology.

5. **Educational Programs for Children and Parents**:

   - **School-Based Initiatives**: Advocating for schools that incorporate digital literacy programs or parental workshops addressing healthy tech habits, aiding both children and parents in navigating technology responsibly.

   - **Parenting Support Groups**: Identifying parenting support groups that focus on managing children's tech usage, offering guidance and shared experiences among parents.

6. **Resource Directories and Hotlines**:

   - **Resource Directories**: Providing access to directories or databases listing local resources, hotlines, or helplines available for individuals seeking guidance or assistance in managing technology use.

   - **24/7 Support Hotlines**: Highlighting available helplines or crisis hotlines specializing in digital wellness issues, offering immediate assistance and guidance when needed.

12. Key Takeaways: Cultivating Healthy Tech Habits within Families

1. **Open Communication and Collaboration**:

   - Fostering open discussions and active listening within families regarding technology use promotes understanding and collaboration in establishing healthy tech habits.

2. **Setting Clear Boundaries**:

   - Establishing clear guidelines and

boundaries around tech use, including tech-free zones or designated screen times, aids in promoting balanced and mindful tech habits.

3. **Modeling Healthy Behavior**:

   • Leading by example and showcasing healthy tech habits by parents and family members influences children to adopt responsible digital practices.

4. **Continuous Adaptation**:

   • Recognizing the evolving nature of technology and adapting habits and rules accordingly ensures that family tech practices remain relevant and conducive to well-being.

5. **Utilizing Support Networks**:

   • Accessing community resources, support groups, and educational platforms aids families in seeking guidance and assistance in maintaining healthy tech habits.

6. **Education and Empowerment**:

   • Equipping both parents and children with digital literacy skills, knowledge about responsible tech use, and access to available resources empowers families to navigate technology mindfully.

7. **Balancing Digital and Offline Activities**:

   • Encouraging a balance between digital engagement and offline activities fosters holistic well-being and meaningful family interactions beyond screens.

8. **Creating a Supportive Environment:**

- Cultivating a supportive and empathetic atmosphere within the family enables discussions, adjustments, and continuous efforts toward maintaining healthy tech habits.

Chapter 8:

Creating Tech-Free Zones and Time Management Techniques

1. Introduction: Establishing Tech-Free Zones and Effective Time Management

In today's digital age, the omnipresence of technology has woven itself seamlessly into our daily lives. Yet, amidst its convenience and connectivity, an excessive reliance on digital devices can often encroach upon vital aspects of our well-being. Chapter 8 delves into a pivotal aspect of recalibrating our relationship with technology: the creation of tech-free zones and the implementation of efficient time management techniques.

Recognizing the Need for Balance

As technology pervades every facet of our existence, finding an equilibrium between its utility and its potential for overconsumption becomes increasingly crucial. The introduction of tech-free zones stands as a proactive measure, carving out sanctuaries within our physical spaces to reclaim moments of uninterrupted human connection, creativity, and relaxation.

Navigating Time in the Digital Epoch

The chapter also traverses the labyrinth of time management in an era characterized by constant connectivity. It explores strategies and methodologies that empower individuals to harness time effectively, curtailing digital distractions to foster a more focused and balanced lifestyle.

Empowering with Strategies

By acknowledging the need for tech-free havens and time allocation strategies, individuals are empowered to regain control over their relationship with technology. This chapter endeavors to equip readers with practical insights, enabling them to carve out spaces and moments that transcend the pervasive influence of digital devices.

Join us on this explorative journey as we navigate the creation of tech-free havens and the cultivation of effective time management practices, aiming to foster a harmonious coexistence with technology in our daily lives.

2. Understanding Tech-Free Zones: Purpose, Benefits, and Implementation

1. **Defining Tech-Free Zones**:

     - **Purposeful Exclusion**: Tech-free zones designate specific physical spaces or times intentionally devoid of digital devices or screens.

     - **Promoting Disconnectivity**: These zones serve as sanctuaries, allowing individuals to disconnect from constant digital stimuli, fostering genuine human interactions, and promoting mindfulness.

2. **Purpose and Objectives**:

     - **Encouraging Present-Mindedness**: Tech-free zones aim to cultivate present-moment awareness, enabling individuals to engage fully in activities without digital distractions.

- **Enhancing Social Interaction**: Creating spaces that encourage face-to-face interactions, deep conversations, and shared experiences among individuals.

3. **Benefits of Tech-Free Zones**:

   - **Restoring Human Connections**: Facilitating meaningful interactions and fostering deeper connections among family members, friends, and colleagues.

   - **Enhanced Creativity and Productivity**: Offering spaces for uninterrupted thought, creativity, and focus, allowing for more productive and innovative thinking.

4. **Areas of Implementation**:

   - **Home Settings**: Designating specific areas at home, such as dining areas, living rooms, or bedrooms, as tech-free zones to encourage family bonding and relaxation.

   - **Work Environments**: Establishing tech-free spaces within workplaces or offices to foster undistracted collaboration, brainstorming, or relaxation zones for employees.

5. **Public Spaces and Institutions**:

   - **Educational Settings**: Implementing tech-free zones in schools, libraries, or educational institutions to encourage focused learning, reading, and social interactions among students.

- **Recreational Areas**: Designating certain public recreational spots, parks, or community centers as tech-free zones to encourage outdoor activities and socialization.

6. **Guidelines and Implementation Strategies**:

- **Clear Guidelines**: Providing clear instructions and guidelines regarding the purpose and usage of tech-free zones to ensure compliance and understanding.

- **Promoting Awareness**: Educating individuals about the benefits and significance of these zones through signage, communication, or awareness campaigns.

3. **Identifying Ideal Tech-Free Spaces: Home, Work, and Educational Environments**

1. **At Home**:

- **Dining Area or Kitchen**: Designating the dining area as a tech-free zone encourages family meals without distractions, fostering meaningful conversations and bonding.

- **Living Room or Common Areas**: Allocating specific corners or zones within living spaces for reading, socializing, or relaxation devoid of digital devices promotes family time and relaxation.

- **Bedroom**: Establishing tech-free bedtime routines in bedrooms aids in improving sleep quality by avoiding screens before sleep.

2. **Work Environments**:

- **Meeting Rooms or Collaboration**

Spaces: Designating certain areas as tech-free during meetings or brainstorming sessions enhances focus, and creativity, and encourages active participation.

- **Designated Break Areas**: Creating tech-free zones in break rooms or relaxation areas allows employees to unwind, fostering social interactions and mental refreshment.

3. **Educational Institutions**:

- **Classrooms and Lecture Halls**: Designating parts of classrooms as tech-free zones during specific educational activities or discussions promotes focused learning and student engagement.

- **Library Spaces**: Allocating sections in libraries as tech-free areas encourage uninterrupted reading, research, and study without digital distractions.

4. **Public Recreational Spaces**:

- **Parks and Playgrounds**: Designating certain areas within public parks or recreational spots as tech-free zones promotes outdoor activities, socialization, and interaction with nature.

- **Community Centers or Clubs**: Creating tech-free spaces within these centers encourages community engagement, face-to-face interactions, and participation in group activities.

5. **Health and Wellness Spaces**:

- **Gyms or Exercise Areas**: Establishing

tech-free zones within fitness centers encourages individuals to focus on their workouts, enhancing concentration and mindfulness during exercises.

- **Meditation or Relaxation Rooms**: Designating specific areas as tech-free zones within wellness centers or spas fosters mental relaxation and mindfulness practices.

6. **Transitional Spaces**:

- **Transit and Commuting**: Encouraging tech-free activities or areas during commuting time, such as reading books or engaging in mindful practices, promotes relaxation and mental rejuvenation.

4. **Establishing Boundaries for Tech-Free Zones: Clear Guidelines and Adherence**

1. **Clarity in Purpose**:

- **Defining Objectives**: Clearly articulate the purpose and benefits of tech-free zones, emphasizing their role in fostering human connection, focused work, or relaxation without digital distractions.

- **Communicating Intentions**: Explain the rationale behind creating these zones to all involved parties, ensuring everyone understands the significance of these spaces.

2. **Designated Areas and Times**:

- **Physical Designation**: Mark or designate the areas where tech-free zones apply, using signage or demarcation to signify these spaces.

- **Scheduled Tech-Free Periods**: Establish specific times or occasions (e.g., meals, meetings, bedtime) when tech-free zones are in effect, ensuring a consistent application of these boundaries.

3. **Consistent Guidelines**:

   - **Consistency in Rules**: Ensure consistency in applying tech-free zone rules across different settings, whether at home, work, educational institutions, or public spaces.

   - **Universal Understanding**: Communicate and reinforce guidelines universally to all individuals involved, emphasizing the collective responsibility to respect these boundaries.

4. **Respect and Compliance**:

   - **Mutual Respect**: Encourage respect for tech-free zones among family members, colleagues, or users in shared spaces, fostering an understanding of the importance of these zones.

   - **Modeling Behavior**: Lead by example, demonstrating adherence to tech-free zone rules to reinforce their significance and encourage compliance among others.

5. **Communication and Reinforcement**:

   - **Regular Reminders**: Reinforce the importance of tech-free zones through periodic reminders, discussions, or signage to maintain awareness and adherence.

- **Open Communication Channels**: Encourage open dialogue regarding the implementation and effectiveness of tech-free zones, allowing for adjustments or improvements based on feedback.

6. **Positive Reinforcement**:

   - **Acknowledgment and Encouragement**: Recognize and appreciate efforts made to adhere to tech-free zone rules, fostering a positive environment that encourages compliance and participation.

5. Benefits of Tech-Free Time: Fostering Focus, Creativity, and Mental Well-being

1. **Enhanced Focus and Productivity**:

   - **Reduced Distractions**: Allocating tech-free periods enables individuals to concentrate better on tasks at hand, minimizing interruptions and improving overall productivity.

   - **Improved Task Completion**: Uninterrupted periods devoid of digital distractions allow for deeper immersion in activities, leading to more efficient and effective task completion.

2. **Boost to Creativity and Innovation**:

   - **Unhindered Thought Processes**: Tech-free time offers mental space for unrestricted thinking, fostering creativity, imagination, and innovative thinking.

   - **Inspired Problem-Solving**: Engaging in tech-free activities encourages novel approaches to problem-solving, facilitating fresh perspectives and out-of-the-box solutions.

3. **Stress Reduction and Mental Clarity**:

   - **Mindful Presence**: Disconnecting from technology promotes mindfulness, reducing stress levels, and fostering mental clarity by offering moments of calm and reflection.

   - **Improved Emotional Well-being**: Tech-free time allows individuals to disconnect from constant stimulation, aiding in emotional regulation and promoting a sense of balance and tranquility.

4. **Enhanced Social Interactions**:

   - **Quality Time with Others**: Allocating tech-free periods encourages genuine face-to-face interactions, strengthening relationships, and deepening social connections.

   - **Improved Communication**: Disconnecting from screens promotes active listening and better communication skills, enhancing the quality of interpersonal relationships.

5. **Better Sleep and Relaxation**:

   - **Improved Sleep Patterns**: Engaging in tech-free activities before bedtime promotes better sleep quality by reducing exposure to blue light, aiding in a more restful night's sleep.

- **Relaxation and Unwinding**: Disconnecting from digital devices during leisure time promotes relaxation, allowing individuals to unwind and de-stress more effectively.

6. **Increased Physical Activity**:

    - **Encouragement of Movement**: Tech-free time encourages engagement in physical activities, hobbies, or outdoor pursuits, promoting a more active and healthier lifestyle.

6. **Strategies for Implementing Tech-Free Time: Practical Approaches for Unplugging**

    1. **Schedule Device-Free Periods**:

        - **Designated Hours**: Allocate specific hours or time slots daily/weekly for tech-free activities, such as during meals, evenings, or weekends, fostering uninterrupted personal or family time.

        - **Digital Detox Days**: Designate occasional full days or weekends as 'digital detox' periods, where individuals or families abstain from digital devices entirely.

    2. **Create Tech-Free Zones or Spaces**:

        - **Physical Boundaries**: Designate certain areas within homes or workplaces as tech-free zones, encouraging activities like reading, hobbies, or conversation without digital distractions.

        - **Establish Screen-Free Bedrooms**: Encourage a screen-free environment in bedrooms to promote relaxation, better sleep, and healthier bedtime routines.

3. **Unplugged Activities and Hobbies**:

   - **Engage in Analog Activities**: Encourage hobbies or pastimes that don't involve screens, such as reading physical books, arts, and crafts, or outdoor activities like hiking or gardening.

   - **Family Bonding Time**: Plan tech-free activities like board games, sports, or outings that encourage family members or friends to engage without relying on devices.

4. **Mindful Practices**:

   - **Practice Mindfulness**: Incorporate mindfulness or meditation sessions into tech-free time to encourage relaxation, self-reflection, and mental clarity.

   - **Mindful Eating**: Promote device-free meals, encouraging individuals to savor food, engage in meaningful conversations, and be fully present during mealtimes.

5. **Limit Screen Use Before Bed**:

   - **Establish a Digital Curfew**: Encourage a buffer period before bedtime where screens are avoided, allowing the mind to unwind and prepare for restful sleep.

   - **Adopt Relaxing Activities**: Replace screen time with relaxing pre-sleep rituals like reading a book, gentle stretching, or practicing calming routines.

6. **Set Boundaries and Rules**:

   • **Family Agreements**: Involve family members in creating tech-free rules and agreements, fostering collective responsibility and respect for tech-free periods.

   • **Workplace Guidelines**: Establish tech-free periods during meetings or certain work hours to promote focused collaboration and productivity.

7. **Digital Detox Challenges or Rewards**:

   • **Create Challenges**: Introduce challenges or incentives to reduce screen time, rewarding successful completion with enjoyable non-tech rewards.

   • **Track Progress**: Use apps or trackers that monitor screen time to increase awareness and encourage gradual reduction.

7. **Effective Time Management Techniques: Optimizing Screen Time and Productivity**

   1. **Set Specific Time Limits**:

      • **Time Blocking**: Allocate specific time slots for different activities, including screen time, work, leisure, and breaks, ensuring a balanced approach to tasks.

      • **Use Timers or Alarms**: Set alarms or timers to limit screen time sessions, aiding in self-regulation and preventing excessive usage.

   2. **Utilize Productivity Apps and Tools**:

      • **Task Management Apps**: Use apps or tools that aid in task prioritization, scheduling, and time tracking, enhancing productivity and focus during screen use.

- **Distraction Blockers**: Install apps or browser extensions that block distracting websites or apps during designated work or study periods.

3. **Implement the Pomodoro Technique**:

- **Structured Work Intervals**: Adopt the Pomodoro Technique, working in focused intervals (e.g., 25 minutes) followed by short breaks, maximizing productivity and maintaining focus.

4. **Prioritize Tasks and Activities**:

- **Eisenhower Matrix**: Use this matrix to categorize tasks based on urgency and importance, prioritizing high-value activities over less critical ones during screen time.

- **To-Do Lists**: Create daily or weekly to-do lists, organizing tasks by priority and ensuring a clear focus on essential activities during screen sessions.

5. **Practice Time Batching**:

- **Group Similar Tasks**: Batch similar activities together during screen time, optimizing efficiency by reducing context-switching and increasing concentration on related tasks.

6. **Establish Tech-Free Time Intervals**:

- **Digital Sabbaticals**: Introduce intervals during the day or week where screens are entirely avoided, allowing for dedicated focus on non-screen activities or rest.

7. **Mindful Screen Use:**

- **Intentional Screen Engagement**: Practice intentional use of screens by setting clear objectives for each session, and avoiding aimless scrolling or browsing.

- **Focused Work Periods**: Allocate uninterrupted blocks of time for deep work or focused tasks, minimizing distractions and optimizing productivity during screen use.

8. **Reflect and Adjust:**

- **Regular Evaluation**: Assess screen time habits periodically, reflecting on productivity and adjusting strategies based on effectiveness and personal preferences.

- **Flexibility and Adaptation**: Remain flexible in modifying time management techniques to suit evolving needs or circumstances for optimal productivity.

8. **Utilizing Technology for Time Management: Tools and Apps**

1. **Calendar and Scheduling Apps:**

- **Google Calendar, Outlook, or Apple Calendar**: These platforms allow scheduling tasks, setting reminders, and organizing events, ensuring efficient time allocation and task prioritization.

- **Scheduling Tools**: Apps like Doodle or Calendly aid in scheduling meetings, managing appointments, and coordinating availability among multiple parties.

2. **Task and Project Management Apps**:

   - **Todoist, Trello, Asana**: These apps assist in organizing tasks, setting deadlines, and tracking progress, enhancing productivity and collaboration across projects or teams.

   - **Notion or Evernote**: Versatile platforms for note-taking, project management, and task organization, allowing customization to suit individual preferences.

3. **Focus and Distraction Control Apps**:

   - **Forest or Focus@Will**: These apps help maintain focus and limit distractions by using techniques like the Pomodoro Method or providing focused music for concentration.

   - **Freedom or Cold Turkey**: Tools that block distracting websites or apps during specified periods, reducing temptation and promoting focused work sessions.

4. **Time Tracking and Analytics Tools**:

   - **RescueTime or Toggl**: Track time spent on various tasks or apps, providing insights into productivity patterns, aiding in identifying time sinks, and optimizing efficiency.

   - **Clockify or Harvest**: Track billable hours, create timesheets, and analyze time allocation for different projects or clients, aiding in time management for freelancers or businesses.

5. **Automation and AI-Assisted Tools**:

   - **IFTTT or Zapier**: Automate

repetitive tasks or create task triggers across different apps, saving time and streamlining workflows.

- **AI-Powered Assistants**: Tools like Siri, Google Assistant, or Alexa can set reminders, manage schedules, and provide assistance in organizing tasks using voice commands.

6. **Goal Tracking and Habit Building Apps**:

- **Strides or Habitica**: Track goals, build habits, and maintain consistency by visualizing progress and setting milestones, promoting self-accountability and time management.

7. **Collaboration and Communication Tools**:

- **Slack, Microsoft Teams, or Zoom**: Facilitate efficient communication and collaboration among teams, reducing time spent on unnecessary meetings or long email threads.

8. **Smartphone Features and Settings**:

- **Focus Mode or Screen Time**: Utilize built-in features that limit app usage, enforce tech breaks, or block distractions, enhancing mindful screen use and time management.

9. **Mindful Tech Consumption: Cultivating Awareness in Digital Engagement**

1. **Mindful Awareness**:

- **Pause and Reflect**: Before engaging with technology, take a moment to pause, breathe, and reflect on your intention behind using the device or app.

- **Mindful Entry and Exit**: Consciously enter and exit digital engagements, being aware of your emotional state and purpose for using the technology.

2. **Establish Tech-Free Rituals**:

- **Mindful Transitions**: Designate moments in your day for tech-free transitions, such as the first and last hour of the day, fostering calm and focused starts and ends.

- **Mindful Breaks**: Incorporate short breaks between digital activities, using them to stretch, breathe, or engage in non-screen activities mindfully.

3. **Practice Digital Mindfulness**:

- **Focused Engagement**: While using technology, maintain focus on the present task or content, avoiding multitasking to enhance attention and depth of engagement.

- **Mindful Responses**: Consciously respond rather than react to notifications or digital stimuli, considering if and how they align with your intentions.

4. **Mindful Notifications and Settings**:

- **Notification Awareness**: Review and customize notification settings, allowing only essential alerts, reducing distractions, and promoting mindful usage.

- **Scheduled Tech Time**: Set specific times for checking emails, social media, or specific apps, limiting impulsive and excessive usage.

5. **Digital Detox and Unplugging**:

   - **Mindful Detox Periods**: Plan periodic digital detoxes or screen-free days/weekends, allowing time for introspection, relaxation, and face-to-face interactions.

   - **Tech-Free Zones**: Designate certain areas in your environment as tech-free zones, fostering spaces for mindfulness, relaxation, or family engagement without screens.

6. **Mindful Consumption Habits**:

   - **Conscious Content Selection**: Choose digital content mindfully, opting for quality and beneficial material, avoiding mindless scrolling or consumption.

   - **Reflective Use**: After digital engagements, take a moment to reflect on the experience, evaluating its impact on your well-being and mental state.

7. **Mindfulness Practices Integration**:

   - **Mindful Breathing**: Practice brief breathing exercises or mindful moments before or after using technology, promoting relaxation and mental clarity.

   - **Mindful Movement**: Incorporate mindful movement or stretching during tech breaks to counteract the sedentary nature of screen time.

8. **Regular Mindfulness Exercises**:

   - **Mindfulness Apps**: Utilize apps offering guided mindfulness practices or meditation, fostering awareness and mental balance amidst digital engagements.

10. **Striking a Balance: Cultivating Tech Use Harmony**

1. **Set Clear Boundaries**:

   - **Define Tech-Free Periods**: Establish dedicated tech-free times, such as during meals, before bedtime, or during family gatherings, fostering genuine connections and relaxation.

   - **Tech-Free Zones**: Designate specific areas in your home or workspace as tech-free zones, encouraging mindful and tech-free activities.

2. **Prioritize Purposeful Use**:

   - **Intentional Tech Consumption**: Align tech use with specific purposes, such as work-related tasks, learning, communication, or genuine leisure, avoiding mindless scrolling or excessive browsing.

   - **Productivity vs. Leisure**: Segment tech use for productivity and leisure separately, ensuring distinct time allocation for work-related activities and recreational engagement.

3. **Mindful Tech Integration**:

   - **Mindful Multitasking**: Avoid excessive multitasking, focusing on one task at a time to enhance efficiency and reduce distractions.

- **Tech-Assisted Leisure**: Utilize technology for meaningful leisure activities, such as learning new skills, creative pursuits, or hobbies, promoting productive relaxation.

4. **Regular Tech Breaks**:

- **Scheduled Tech Breaks**: Incorporate regular breaks from technology throughout the day, fostering mental refreshment and reducing screen fatigue.

- **Tech-Free Activities**: Engage in offline activities, hobbies, or physical exercises during breaks, balancing screen time with rejuvenating non-screen activities.

5. **Evaluate and Adjust**:

- **Periodic Assessments**: Regularly evaluate your tech use habits and their impact on your well-being, making adjustments to restore balance if necessary.

- **Flexible Guidelines**: Be adaptable with tech use guidelines, allowing for flexibility while ensuring they align with your well-being goals.

6. **Quality Over Quantity**:

- **Curate Content**: Prioritize quality over quantity when consuming digital content, focusing on informative, enriching, and meaningful material, minimizing mindless scrolling.

- **Balanced Information Diet**: Maintain a balanced information diet, diversifying the sources and types of content consumed for a well-rounded perspective.

7. **Family and Social Agreements**:

- **Family Discussions**: Engage in open discussions with family members about tech use agreements, setting collective guidelines to foster balanced tech consumption.

- **Social Engagement Prioritization**: Prioritize face-to-face interactions and offline activities in social settings, nurturing real connections beyond virtual engagements.

8. **Self-Reflection and Adjustment**:

- **Reflective Practices**: Regularly reflect on your tech habits, assessing their impact on your overall well-being, and make conscious adjustments as needed for a more balanced approach.

11. **Tracking and Evaluating Tech Usage Patterns**

1. **Usage Tracking Tools**:

- **Apps and Software**: Utilize apps or software designed for tracking screen time and digital usage across devices, offering insights into daily usage patterns.

- **Activity Logs**: Maintain a personal activity log or journal to record the time and purpose behind each tech interaction, allowing for self-reflection.

2. **Quantify Screen Time**:

- **Time Analytics**: Use time analytics features available in devices or apps to quantify time spent on different activities, categorizing them for better analysis.

- **Weekly or Monthly Review**: Regularly review usage data on a weekly or monthly basis, identifying trends and areas for improvement.

3. **Identify Usage Trends**:

- **Peak Usage Times**: Identify peak usage times during the day or week, understanding when tech usage is highest or most prevalent.

- **Frequency of App Usage**: Track the frequency of app or platform usage, noting the apps most frequently accessed and the time spent on each.

4. **Purposeful vs. Mindless Usage**:

- **Purposeful vs. Passive**: Distinguish between purposeful tech usages, such as work-related tasks or intentional leisure, and passive, mindless scrolling or browsing.

- **Productivity Analysis**: Evaluate the impact of tech use on productivity, noting whether certain activities enhance or hinder your productivity.

5. **Impact on Well-being**:

- **Emotional Impact**: Reflect on the emotional impact of tech use, identifying how certain activities affect your mood, stress levels, and overall well-being.

- **Physical Considerations**: Consider physical effects, such as eye strain or posture issues, stemming from prolonged tech use.

6. **Set Improvement Goals**:

- **Identify Areas for Improvement**: Based on the evaluation, pinpoint specific areas where you aim to reduce or optimize tech usage for a more balanced routine.

- **Goal Setting**: Set realistic and achievable goals, such as reducing screen time during certain hours or allocating more time to offline activities.

7. **Review and Adjust**:

- **Regular Review**: Consistently review your progress towards usage improvement goals, adjusting strategies or habits accordingly for continual improvement.

- **Flexibility in Approaches**: Stay open to adjusting tracking methods or goals based on evolving needs and experiences.

8. **Seek External Feedback**:

- **Peer Input or Support**: Consider seeking feedback from trusted peers or family members on your tech usage habits, gaining an external perspective for improvement.

12. **Key Takeaways**

1. **Purposeful Tech-Free Zones**:

- Designating specific areas or periods as tech-free encourages focused, non-digital activities, fostering mental clarity and promoting deeper connections.

2. **Benefits of Tech-Free Time**:

- Allocating time away from screens fosters improved concentration, boosts creativity, and contributes to better mental and emotional well-being.

3. **Setting Clear Boundaries**:

- Establishing guidelines for tech-free zones within homes, workplaces, and educational spaces helps maintain a healthy balance between digital and non-digital activities.

4. **Effective Time Management**:

- Implementing time management techniques allows for better control over screen time, prioritizing tasks, and allocating specific periods for productive, leisure, and tech-free activities.

5. **Mindful Consumption**:

- Integrating mindfulness into tech use fosters awareness, encouraging intentional consumption and reducing mindless browsing or excessive screen time.

6. **Balancing Offline Activities**:

- Engaging in offline hobbies, physical activities, and face-to-face interactions provides a holistic lifestyle, supplementing tech usage with enriching non-digital experiences.

7. **Continuous Evaluation and Adaptation**:

- Regularly tracking tech usage patterns, evaluating their impact, and adjusting strategies ensure ongoing improvement towards a balanced tech lifestyle.

8. **Family and Community Engagement:**

- Involving family members and communities in creating tech-free zones fosters collective responsibility and encourages healthier tech habits for all.

IV.

De-Addiction Measures

Chapter 9:

Mindfulness and Mental Health Approaches

1. Introduction

In an era characterized by ubiquitous technology, the pursuit of mental well-being amidst the digital chaos has become increasingly imperative. This chapter delves into the transformative power of mindfulness as a tool to navigate the complexities of technology addiction and promote mental health.

Mindfulness in the Digital Age

Mindfulness, rooted in ancient practices, has emerged as a beacon of hope in the modern digital age. Its essence lies in cultivating present-moment awareness, fostering a conscious relationship with one's thoughts, emotions, and surroundings. Amidst the incessant distractions of technology, mindfulness serves as a refuge, offering a pathway to reclaim mental clarity and emotional balance.

Addressing Mental Health Challenges

The relentless use of technology often intertwines with mental health challenges, including stress, anxiety, and depression. Mindfulness practices, when integrated into daily life, equip individuals with tools to navigate these challenges. By fostering self-awareness and resilience, mindfulness becomes a catalyst for improved mental health outcomes in the face of technological inundation.

Technology and Mindful Consumption

Moreover, this chapter explores the synergy between technology and mindful consumption. It unveils strategies to leverage technology as a facilitator of mindfulness, rather than a hindrance, emphasizing the role of digital resources in fostering mental well-being.

A Holistic Approach

Embracing a holistic approach, this chapter ventures beyond the superficialities of mindfulness, delving into its profound impact on rewiring cognitive patterns, managing emotions, and nurturing mental resilience. It envisions a landscape where technology and mindfulness coexist harmoniously, contributing synergistically to mental health enhancement.

Empowering Mental Well-being

Ultimately, this chapter aspires to empower individuals with the tools of mindfulness, acknowledging its transformative potential in fostering mental well-being amid the pervasive influence of technology. It endeavors to guide readers on a transformative journey toward harnessing mindfulness as a shield against the perils of digital overload.

2. Understanding Mindfulness

Definition: Mindfulness encapsulates a state of being fully present and engaged in the current moment, acknowledging thoughts, sensations, emotions, and surroundings without judgment or attachment. It embodies an intentional and non-reactive awareness of one's experiences.

Core Principles:

1. **Present-Moment Awareness**: Mindfulness emphasizes redirecting attention to the present moment, focusing on the "here and now" rather than

dwelling on the past or anticipating the future.

2. Non-Judgmental Acceptance: It involves observing thoughts and feelings impartially, without labeling them as good or bad. This non-judgmental stance encourages acceptance of experiences as they arise.

3. Cultivation of Intentionality: Mindfulness involves the deliberate cultivation of intentionality in actions, thoughts, and responses, fostering a conscious approach to daily life.

4. Focused Attention: It encourages directing attention purposefully, whether on sensations in the body, the breath, or the immediate environment, fostering concentration and mental clarity.

Role in Daily Life:

Mindfulness practices encompass various techniques such as meditation, deep breathing exercises, body scans, and mindful movements. When integrated into daily routines, mindfulness becomes a tool for reducing stress, enhancing emotional regulation, and fostering mental resilience.

Application in the Digital Age:

In the context of technology addiction and the digital age, mindfulness serves as a counterbalance. It offers individuals a means to detach from the constant stimuli of technology, fostering a sense of calm amidst the digital chaos.

Benefits:

Embracing mindfulness practices yields numerous benefits, including stress reduction, improved focus and attention, increased emotional intelligence, and a greater sense of overall well-being.

3. **Mindfulness Practices**

Meditation:

- **Focused Attention Meditation**: This involves concentrating on a single point of focus, such as the breath, a specific sensation, or a mantra, training the mind to remain present.

- **Open Monitoring Meditation**: It involves non-reactively observing thoughts, emotions, and sensations as they arise without attachment or judgment.

Deep Breathing Exercises:

- **Diaphragmatic Breathing**: Focusing on deep, intentional breathing patterns that engage the diaphragm, promoting relaxation and reducing stress.

- **Box Breathing or 4-7-8 Breathing**: Inhaling for a count of four, holding for seven, and exhaling for eight, creating a calming effect on the nervous system.

Mindful Observation:

- **Body Scan**: A practice involving systematically directing attention through different parts of the body, noticing sensations without trying to change them.

- **Mindful Eating**: Paying full attention to the act of eating, savoring each bite, and being aware of the sensory experiences associated with eating.

Mindful Movement:

- **Yoga**: Engaging in yoga poses mindfully, syncing breath with movement, promoting physical well-being while enhancing present-moment awareness.

- **Walking Meditation**: Practicing walking slowly and deliberately, paying attention to each step, sensations in the feet, and the surrounding environment.

Implementation Guidance:

- **Starting Small**: Beginning with short sessions, gradually increasing duration as comfort and familiarity with the practice grow.

- **Consistency**: Regular practice, even for a few minutes each day, is more beneficial than sporadic longer sessions.

- **Non-Judgmental Observation**: Encouraging an open and non-judgmental approach towards experiences during practice, allowing thoughts and feelings to arise without criticism.

Integration into Daily Life:

- **Mindful Transitions**: Incorporating mindfulness into daily transitions like waking up, commuting, or transitioning between tasks.

- **Technology-Free Mindfulness**: Carving out moments for mindfulness without the interference of digital devices, allowing for uninterrupted self-reflection.

Customization:

- **Personal Preferences**: Encouraging individuals to explore and find practices that resonate with their preferences, allowing for a more sustainable and enjoyable experience.

4. Mindfulness in the Digital Age

Relevance in a Technology-Driven Society:

In today's technology-driven society, the incessant influx of digital stimuli challenges our capacity for sustained attention and emotional regulation. Mindfulness emerges as a crucial tool, offering a counterbalance to the distractions and overstimulation brought about by technology.

Cultivating Presence Amidst Digital Chaos:

Mindfulness acts as an anchor amidst the chaos of notifications, social media, and constant connectivity. It encourages individuals to pause, disconnect from the digital realm, and reconnect with the present moment. This intentional disconnection fosters mental clarity and emotional stability.

Combatting Digital Overwhelm:

The barrage of information and the continuous demand for attention in the digital sphere often lead to feelings of being overwhelmed and stressed. Mindfulness practices provide individuals with a refuge, enabling them to create mental space, reduce stress, and regain a sense of control amid the digital cacophony.

Enhancing Digital Engagement:

Ironically, mindfulness also enhances the quality of digital engagement. Encouraging individuals to approach technology with conscious awareness, fosters deliberate and meaningful interactions. This conscious approach to digital consumption leads to more intentional and fulfilling online experiences.

Fostering Mental Well-being:

The integration of mindfulness practices into daily life offers an antidote to the potential negative impacts of technology on mental health. It empowers individuals to manage stress, anxiety, and digital fatigue, promoting mental resilience and overall well-being.

Balancing Technology and Mindfulness:

Mindfulness doesn't advocate for complete detachment from technology but rather encourages a mindful relationship with it. It prompts individuals to approach technology with a sense of awareness, intentionality, and moderation, creating a healthier balance in digital consumption.

Cultivating Mindful Tech Habits:

Incorporating mindfulness into daily tech habits involves conscious decisions such as setting boundaries, practicing tech-free moments, and infusing mindfulness into digital interactions. This integration fosters a harmonious coexistence between technology and mindful living.

5. Mindfulness and Stress Reduction

Awareness of Digital Stressors:

Mindfulness techniques equip individuals with the ability to recognize the stressors inherent in excessive technology use. This awareness allows them to identify triggers, such as constant notifications or social comparison, leading to stress and anxiety.

Mindful Response to Stress:

Mindfulness practices cultivate a non-reactive, observant stance towards stressors encountered in the digital realm. Instead of reacting impulsively or becoming overwhelmed, individuals develop the capacity to respond calmly and consciously to technological stressors.

Stress Reduction through Mindful Practices:

- **Breathing Techniques**: Mindful breathing exercises serve as immediate stress alleviators, calming the nervous system and reducing the physiological response to stress triggered by technology-induced tension.

- **Meditation and Relaxation**: Regular meditation sessions or relaxation exercises offer a dedicated space to unwind from the digital world, reducing stress and anxiety accumulated throughout the day.

- **Digital Detoxing**: Mindfulness prompts individuals to engage in intentional digital detoxes, disconnecting from screens and technology to reset and alleviate stress caused by constant connectivity.

Promotion of Emotional Regulation:

Mindfulness fosters emotional regulation, enabling individuals to manage emotions triggered by technology-induced stress. It encourages a compassionate self-awareness that helps navigate feelings of frustration, comparison, or information overload commonly experienced in digital environments.

Mindful Coping Strategies:

- **Mindful Distraction**: Using mindfulness techniques as a positive distraction from digital stressors, redirecting focus to the present moment to alleviate stress and anxiety caused by technology.

- **Digital Boundaries**: Establishing mindful boundaries around technology use, setting specific time limits, or creating tech-free zones to reduce the stress of continuous digital engagement.

Improved Cognitive Responses:

Mindfulness practices enhance cognitive flexibility and resilience, helping individuals adapt to the fast-paced nature of digital interactions. This allows for better problem-solving and reduces the tendency to feel overwhelmed by the constant influx of information.

Overall Well-being Promotion:

By reducing stress and promoting mental resilience, mindfulness supports overall well-being, allowing individuals to enjoy the benefits of technology while mitigating its adverse effects on mental health.

6. Mindful Tech Consumption

Conscious Awareness of Digital Engagement:

Mindful tech consumption begins with conscious awareness of one's interaction with digital devices. It involves acknowledging the purpose and duration of device usage before engaging, promoting intentionality in the digital realm.

Intentional Engagement:

Mindful tech consumption encourages individuals to approach digital devices with clear intentions. It involves asking purposeful questions before engaging with technology, such as "Why am I using this device?" or "What am I seeking to achieve or gain from this interaction?"

Setting Clear Intentions and Goals:

Establishing clear intentions and goals for technology use fosters mindful engagement. Whether it's for work, learning, relaxation, or social interaction, setting specific objectives helps individuals stay focused and avoid aimless browsing or usage.

Scheduled Tech Time:

Practicing scheduled tech time involves setting dedicated periods for digital engagement while also incorporating deliberate breaks or tech-free intervals. This approach allows for mindful allocation of time to digital activities without overindulgence.

Mindful Tech Check-Ins:

Encouraging intermittent tech check-ins throughout the day fosters mindfulness. Pausing at intervals to assess one's digital interactions helps in evaluating whether device usage aligns with predetermined intentions and goals.

Mindful Transitioning:

Mindful transitions between digital and non-digital activities involve consciously moving from one realm to another. This practice includes engaging in grounding activities like deep breathing or setting intentions before transitioning between digital and offline moments.

7. Practicing Gratitude and Reflection

After digital interactions, reflecting on the experience and expressing gratitude for the benefits gained or lessons learned encourages mindfulness. This reflection promotes awareness of the impact of technology use on mental state and productivity.

Limiting Multitasking:

Mindful tech consumption discourages multitasking and encourages focused, single-task engagement. It involves dedicating full attention to a single digital task, promoting depth over superficial engagement.

Regular Digital Detoxes:

Periodic digital detoxes, where individuals intentionally disconnect from devices for set durations, promote mindful tech consumption. These breaks allow for mental rejuvenation and reflection on the impact of technology on daily life.

8. Cultivating Digital Detox Practices

Understanding Digital Detox:

Introducing the concept of digital detox involves taking

intentional breaks from digital devices to reset, recharge, and create a healthier relationship with technology.

Benefits of Digital Detox:

- **Mental Reset**: Digital detox allows the mind to unwind from constant digital stimulation, promoting mental clarity and reducing stress.

- **Improved Focus**: Detoxing from screens can enhance focus and concentration, allowing for deeper engagement in offline activities.

- **Enhanced Relationships**: Disconnecting from technology fosters more meaningful face-to-face interactions, strengthening personal connections.

Setting Detox Goals:

Encouraging individuals to define their digital detox goals helps create a clear purpose for the break. Whether it's a full day, weekend, or periodic shorter intervals, setting achievable detox goals is crucial.

Establishing Detox Periods:

Designating specific times for digital detox, whether daily, weekly, or monthly, creates a routine. It might involve evenings, weekends, or certain days dedicated to tech-free activities.

Creating Tech-Free Zones:

Designating physical spaces as tech-free zones promotes a conducive environment for detox periods. Areas like bedrooms or dining spaces can be designated as tech-free to encourage face-to-face interactions and relaxation.

Alternative Activities:

Encouraging individuals to engage in offline activities during digital detoxes, such as reading, exercising, practicing hobbies, or spending time in nature, promotes a healthy balance.

Mindful Planning for Detoxes:

Mindful planning involves scheduling detox periods in advance, notifying peers or family members about the break, and mentally preparing to disconnect.

Gradual Implementation:

For those accustomed to heavy digital usage, gradual implementation of digital detoxes can be more effective. Starting with shorter detox periods and gradually extending the duration can ease the transition.

Managing Expectations:

Managing expectations around digital detox is important. Acknowledging potential discomfort or FOMO (fear of missing out) during detoxes while focusing on the long-term benefits can make the experience more manageable.

Reflection and Adjustment:

Encouraging reflection after each digital detox period allows individuals to evaluate their experiences, adjust strategies, and reinforce positive aspects of the break.

9. **Mental Health Support for Technology Addiction**

    Cognitive-Behavioral Therapy (CBT):

    - **Identifying Triggers**: CBT helps individuals recognize thought patterns and behaviors associated with technology addiction. Therapists work with patients to identify triggers and develop coping strategies.

    - **Behavioral Modification**: Through CBT, individuals learn to modify their behaviors by replacing negative habits with healthier alternatives. This may involve setting limits on device usage, gradually reducing screen time, and managing impulses.

Mindfulness-Based Interventions:

- **Mindfulness Practices**: Incorporating mindfulness into therapy sessions or as standalone interventions aids in developing awareness and self-regulation. Mindfulness techniques help individuals manage urges to compulsively use technology.

- **Stress Reduction**: Mindfulness practices reduce stress and promote emotional regulation, assisting individuals in dealing with the anxiety and restlessness often associated with technology addiction.

Family Therapy:

- **Improving Communication**: Involving family members in therapy sessions can foster open communication and understanding. Family therapy helps in addressing familial dynamics influenced by technology overuse and establishes healthier norms.

Support Groups and Peer Support:

- **Community Engagement**: Support groups, both in-person and online, provide a sense of community and shared experiences. Peer support offers empathy, encouragement, and practical tips for managing technology addiction.

Experiential Therapies:

- **Art or Movement Therapy**: Experiential therapies, like art or movement-based therapies, provide alternative means of expression and stress relief, serving as effective complements to traditional talk therapy.

Psychoeducation and Skill-Building:

- **Understanding Addiction**: Psychoeducation on addiction and its neurological and psychological aspects helps individuals comprehend the nature of their behavior and empowers them to take control.

Holistic Approaches:

- **Healthy Lifestyle Integration**: Therapeutic approaches may also involve integrating healthy lifestyle habits such as exercise, nutrition, and sleep hygiene to support overall mental well-being.

Tailored Treatment Plans:

- **Individualized Approach**: Effective treatment plans are tailored to each individual's needs, considering their specific technology usage patterns, mental health concerns, and personal circumstances.

10. Promoting Emotional Well-being through Mindfulness

Emotional Regulation:

- **Awareness of Emotional Triggers**: Mindfulness fosters awareness of emotional triggers associated with technology use, enabling individuals to recognize and manage emotional responses effectively.

- **Cultivating Emotional Awareness**: Mindfulness practices encourage individuals to observe emotions without judgment, allowing for a better understanding of their feelings and responses to technology-related stressors.

Stress Reduction:

- **Mindful Coping Strategies**: Mindfulness techniques like deep breathing, meditation, or body scans can serve as effective coping strategies to manage stress arising from constant digital engagement.

- **Resilience Building**: Regular mindfulness practice enhances resilience by promoting a non-reactive, more adaptable response to stressors related to technology, improving emotional fortitude.

Enhanced Well-being:

- **Emotional Balance**: Mindfulness cultivates a sense of emotional balance by fostering a more measured and controlled response to technological stressors, reducing emotional volatility.

- **Improved Self-awareness**: Mindfulness encourages self-reflection, aiding individuals in understanding their emotional states, needs, and limits concerning technology use.

Reduced Anxiety and Overwhelm:

- **Anxiety Management**: Mindfulness practices mitigate anxiety by promoting a present-centered focus, reducing worries about past technology-related experiences or future consequences.

- **Calm Amidst Overstimulation**: Mindfulness enables individuals to find moments of calm and peace amidst the constant stimulation from technology, aiding in managing feelings of being overwhelmed.

Improved Relationships:

- **Enhanced Empathy and Connection**: Mindfulness practices foster empathy and deeper connections by encouraging individuals to be present and attentive in interpersonal interactions beyond technology.

Integration into Daily Life:

- **Regular Practice**: Integrating mindfulness practices into daily routines establishes emotional regulation habits, allowing individuals to navigate technology-related stressors more effectively.

11. Building Resilience and Coping Mechanisms through Mindfulness

Resilience Development:

- **Adaptability and Flexibility**: Mindfulness fosters adaptability by encouraging individuals to acknowledge and accept challenges associated with technology addiction, fostering a more flexible mindset.

- **Embracing Impermanence**: Mindfulness practices teach individuals to acknowledge the transient nature of discomfort or urges related to technology addiction, cultivating resilience in the face of these impulses.

Coping Mechanisms:

- **Stress Reduction Techniques**: Mindfulness provides a toolkit of stress reduction techniques—such as mindful breathing, meditation, or body scans—that serve as coping mechanisms during challenging moments of technology craving or overuse.

- **Non-reactive Response**: Mindfulness encourages a non-reactive response to triggers associated with technology addiction, allowing individuals to observe impulses without acting on them impulsively.

Mindful Decision-making:

- **Thoughtful Responses**: Practicing

mindfulness facilitates more thoughtful decision-making when faced with technology-related triggers, promoting considered responses rather than impulsive reactions.

- **Strengthening Self-control**: Mindfulness helps in cultivating self-control, empowering individuals to make intentional choices about their technology use rather than succumbing to addictive behaviors impulsively.

Cultivating Mindful Habits:

- **Consistent Practice**: Regular mindfulness practice establishes habits that aid in managing urges and cravings related to technology addiction, promoting a more mindful approach to daily digital interactions.

Stress Resilience:

- **Reduced Reactivity to Stressors**: Mindfulness promotes a calmer response to stressors associated with technology use, reducing the likelihood of succumbing to stress-induced behaviors.

- **Enhanced Coping Strategies**: Individuals learn to employ effective coping strategies rooted in mindfulness, providing a healthier means of dealing with challenges arising from technology addiction.

Emotional Regulation:

- **Emotional Stability**: Mindfulness fosters emotional regulation, enabling individuals to maintain stability amidst the emotional turmoil often associated with technology addiction.

12. Community Support for Technology Addiction

Peer Support Networks:

- **Shared Experiences**: Community support networks provide a platform for individuals to share their experiences, challenges, and successes in managing technology addiction, fostering a sense of understanding and solidarity.

- **Peer Understanding**: Interacting with peers who have faced similar challenges offers a sense of validation and empathy, reducing feelings of isolation commonly associated with technology addiction.

Mindfulness Groups:

- **Shared Practice**: Mindfulness groups offer a shared space for practicing mindfulness techniques specifically tailored to address technology addiction, promoting a supportive environment for mindfulness-based coping strategies.

- **Guidance and Education**: These groups often provide guidance and education on mindfulness practices targeted at mitigating addictive behaviors linked to technology overuse.

Mental Health Resources:

- **Professional Guidance**: Access to mental health professionals specializing in addiction or mindfulness-based therapies offers individuals tailored support and guidance in managing technology addiction.

- **Therapeutic Intervention**: Counseling, cognitive-behavioral therapy (CBT), or mindfulness-based interventions provided by mental health resources can equip individuals with effective tools to address underlying issues contributing to technology addiction.

Online Communities and Forums:

- **Accessible Support**: Online communities and forums serve as accessible resources where individuals can seek advice, share insights, and find encouragement from others navigating similar challenges related to technology addiction.

- **24/7 Accessibility**: These platforms offer round-the-clock access to support, providing immediate assistance and a sense of community during moments of distress or urgency.

Local Support Groups:

- **Physical Meetups**: Local support groups allow for face-to-face interactions, fostering a sense of belonging and community among individuals seeking assistance with technology addiction.

- **Resource Sharing**: These groups often share local mental health resources, workshops, or seminars tailored to managing addiction in a community setting.

13. **Key Takeaways: Mindfulness and Mental Health Approaches for Technology Addiction**

1. **Mindfulness's Role**: Mindfulness practices serve as potent tools in managing technology addiction by fostering awareness, intentional behavior, and stress reduction in the digital age.

2. **Mental Health Integration**: Integrating mental health approaches, such as counseling, mindfulness-based therapies, and support groups, proves instrumental in aiding individuals struggling

with technology addiction.

3. Stress Reduction and Coping: Mindfulness techniques offer effective stress reduction and coping mechanisms, empowering individuals to navigate the challenges associated with technology overuse.

4. Community and Support: Access to community support networks, mindfulness groups, and mental health resources significantly contributes to managing technology addiction, providing crucial guidance and empathy.

5. Overall Well-being: Emphasizing mindfulness and mental health approaches not only addresses technology addiction but also promotes overall emotional, psychological, and social well-being.

6. Holistic Approach: Adopting a holistic approach that integrates mindfulness, mental health resources, and community support networks offers a comprehensive strategy for individuals seeking to manage technology addiction.

Chapter 10:

Seeking Support: Therapy and Counselling Options

1. Introduction: Seeking Support for Technology Addiction

In the realm of technology addiction, seeking professional support through therapy and counseling stands as a crucial step toward recovery and establishing healthier tech habits. This chapter delves into the significance of these interventions, outlining various therapy options and counseling approaches tailored to address the complexities of technology addiction.

Navigating Technology Addiction Challenges: Acknowledging the multifaceted challenges posed by technology addiction is the initial step toward seeking assistance. Whether grappling with excessive screen time, social media dependency, or gaming addictions, professional guidance provides tailored strategies for each unique circumstance.

Understanding Therapeutic Interventions: Therapy and counseling options offer diverse therapeutic interventions, ranging from cognitive-behavioral therapy (CBT) to specialized addiction counseling. Each approach aims to uncover underlying causes, modify behaviors, and equip individuals with tools to manage and overcome technology addiction.

Exploring Effective Counseling Models: This chapter delves into various counseling models proven effective in treating technology addiction. It examines approaches that blend cognitive restructuring, mindfulness, and behavioral modification to address addictive behaviors associated with excessive technology use.

Role of Professionals in Recovery: Professionals specializing in addiction and mental health play a pivotal role in offering guidance, support, and evidence-based interventions to individuals seeking to reclaim control over their relationship with technology.

Tailored Strategies for Individuals and Families: Therapy and counseling options extend their support not only to individuals but also to families, offering strategies to foster healthier tech habits collectively.

Empowering through Education and Intervention: Offering education, interventions, and personalized guidance, therapy, and counseling empowers individuals to navigate the complexities of technology addiction, fostering resilience and sustainable recovery.

1.1. Recognizing the Need for Professional Help

Technology addiction, with its pervasive influence, often manifests through subtle yet telling signs. Identifying these signs becomes crucial in acknowledging the necessity of professional intervention for effective recovery. This section highlights indicators signaling the imperative need for therapy and counseling in managing technology addiction.

1.2. Signs Indicating Professional Intervention:

1. **Escalating Usage Patterns**: Recognizing a

marked increase in the frequency and duration of technology use beyond one's control.

2. **Neglect of Responsibilities**: Observable neglect or decline in academic, professional, or personal responsibilities due to excessive technology engagement.

3. **Interpersonal Strain**: Noticing strained relationships, social isolation, or withdrawal from meaningful social interactions due to preoccupation with digital devices.

4. **Physical and Emotional Distress**: Experiencing physical symptoms like headaches, eye strain, or emotional distress such as anxiety and mood fluctuations linked to technology use.

5. **Inability to Control Usage**: Inability to regulate or moderate technology usage despite conscious efforts to cut down or control its impact.

1.3. Benefits of Therapy and Counselling:

1. **Tailored Intervention**: Therapy offers individualized strategies to address the specific needs and challenges associated with technology addiction.

2. **Behavioral Modification**: Counseling facilitates behavior modification techniques, empowering individuals to regain control over their technology habits.

3. **Coping Strategies**: Professional assistance equips individuals with coping mechanisms to manage triggers, stressors, and cravings

associated with technology use.

4. **Emotional Support**: Counseling sessions provide a safe space for emotional expression, support, and guidance to navigate the complexities of addiction.

5. **Long-term Recovery**: Therapy and counseling lay the groundwork for sustained recovery, fostering healthier relationships with technology in the long run.

2. **Types of Therapeutic Approaches**

   1. **Cognitive-Behavioral Therapy (CBT)**: CBT stands as a cornerstone in treating technology addiction. It focuses on identifying and modifying thought patterns and behaviors associated with addictive technology use. Through this approach, individuals learn to recognize triggers, challenge distorted beliefs about technology, and develop healthier coping mechanisms.

   2. **Psychotherapy**: Psychotherapy encompasses various modalities like individual therapy, group therapy, and family therapy. It aims to delve into underlying psychological factors contributing to technology addiction. Therapists explore emotional triggers, past experiences, and interpersonal dynamics, aiding individuals in understanding and addressing the root causes of their addictive behaviors.

   3. **Addiction Counseling**: Specialized addiction counseling offers tailored interventions specific to addictive behaviors related to

technology use. It emphasizes behavioral modification techniques, relapse prevention strategies, and tools for managing cravings, fostering sustainable recovery from technology addiction.

4. **Mindfulness-Based Approaches**: Incorporating mindfulness practices, these approaches focus on increasing awareness of one's thoughts, emotions, and behaviors related to technology use. Mindfulness techniques, such as meditation and mindful awareness, help individuals develop a non-judgmental awareness of their relationship with technology.

5. **Family Therapy**: Family therapy involves the participation of family members in the therapeutic process. It addresses how family dynamics, communication patterns, and relationships may contribute to or mitigate technology addiction. This approach fosters a supportive environment and aids in establishing healthy boundaries within the family unit.

6. **Motivational Interviewing (MI)**: MI is a client-centered approach that aims to explore an individual's readiness for change regarding their technology use. By fostering motivation and resolving ambivalence, MI helps individuals recognize the need for change and commit to adopting healthier tech habits.

Each therapeutic approach offers distinct strategies and interventions tailored to the individual's needs, aiding in the management and recovery from technology addiction.

3. Behavioural Modification Techniques

1. **Cognitive-Behavioral Therapy (CBT):** CBT identifies and challenges unhealthy thoughts and behaviors related to technology use. Therapists work with individuals to modify negative thought patterns and develop coping strategies to manage impulses and reduce excessive screen time.

2. **Mindfulness-Based Interventions:** Incorporating mindfulness practices into therapy helps individuals become more aware of their thoughts, emotions, and behaviors around technology. Mindfulness techniques assist in recognizing triggers and fostering a more deliberate and less reactive approach to tech use.

3. **Exposure Therapy:** This method involves gradually exposing individuals to technology triggers in a controlled environment while teaching coping skills to manage cravings or compulsions. Over time, exposure therapy helps desensitize individuals to these triggers.

4. **Contingency Management:** This technique involves reinforcing desired behaviors with rewards or incentives. Therapists may encourage reducing screen time and reward adherence to tech-use goals to reinforce positive changes.

5. **Habit Reversal Training (HRT):** HRT focuses on recognizing and altering habits

associated with technology addiction. Individuals learn to identify triggers, develop competing responses to replace addictive behaviors and practice these alternatives to mitigate the urge to use technology excessively.

6. **Social Skills Training:** For individuals experiencing social isolation due to excessive technology use, therapists conduct training sessions to enhance interpersonal skills, communication strategies, and social interactions to encourage healthier offline connections.

7. **Relapse Prevention Strategies:** Therapists help individuals identify high-risk situations that may lead to relapse and equip them with coping skills to prevent reverting to excessive tech use.

8. **Family-Based Interventions:** In cases where family dynamics contribute to technology addiction, therapists involve family members in therapy sessions to improve communication, establish healthy boundaries, and support the individual's efforts to reduce screen time.

4. **Addressing Underlying Issues**

   1. **Cognitive-Behavioral Therapy (CBT):** CBT identifies and challenges unhealthy thoughts and behaviors related to technology use. Therapists work with individuals to modify negative thought patterns and develop coping strategies to manage impulses and reduce excessive screen time.

   2. **Mindfulness-Based Interventions:**

Incorporating mindfulness practices into therapy helps individuals become more aware of their thoughts, emotions, and behaviors around technology. Mindfulness techniques assist in recognizing triggers and fostering a more deliberate and less reactive approach to tech use.

3. **Exposure Therapy:** This method involves gradually exposing individuals to technology triggers in a controlled environment while teaching coping skills to manage cravings or compulsions. Over time, exposure therapy helps desensitize individuals to these triggers.

4. **Contingency Management:** This technique involves reinforcing desired behaviors with rewards or incentives. Therapists may encourage reducing screen time and reward adherence to tech-use goals to reinforce positive changes.

5. **Habit Reversal Training (HRT):** HRT focuses on recognizing and altering habits associated with technology addiction. Individuals learn to identify triggers, develop competing responses to replace addictive behaviors and practice these alternatives to mitigate the urge to use technology excessively.

6. **Social Skills Training:** For individuals experiencing social isolation due to excessive technology use, therapists conduct training sessions to enhance interpersonal skills, communication strategies, and social interactions to encourage healthier offline

connections.

7. **Relapse Prevention Strategies:** Therapists help individuals identify high-risk situations that may lead to relapse and equip them with coping skills to prevent reverting to excessive tech use.

8. **Family-Based Interventions:** In cases where family dynamics contribute to technology addiction, therapists involve family members in therapy sessions to improve communication, establish healthy boundaries, and support the individual's efforts to reduce screen time.

5. **Family and Group Therapy**

   1. **Family Therapy:** Family therapy involves sessions where the entire family participates to address issues related to technology use. It aims to improve communication, establish healthy boundaries, and promote understanding among family members regarding technology use. It helps identify how family dynamics contribute to addictive behaviors and works on collaborative solutions.

   2. **Group Therapy:** Group sessions involve multiple individuals dealing with technology addiction. These sessions provide a supportive environment where participants can share experiences, struggles, and strategies. It helps in realizing that one is not alone in their struggle and offers peer support and accountability. Group therapy also fosters social connections and interpersonal skills development outside the digital realm.

3. **Social Skills Enhancement:** Both family and group therapies offer opportunities to enhance social skills, communication, and conflict resolution techniques. Individuals learn to interact effectively, build relationships, and manage emotions, reducing the need for excessive reliance on technology for social fulfillment.

4. **Shared Understanding:** In these sessions, individuals or families gain a better understanding of the impact of technology on relationships and daily life. It encourages empathy and enables members to comprehend each other's struggles, facilitating a collective effort towards healthier tech habits.

5. **Setting Mutual Goals:** Family and group therapy sessions often involve setting collective goals for technology use. Establishing shared objectives promotes cooperation, accountability, and a sense of collective responsibility toward maintaining healthy digital boundaries.

6. **Support and Encouragement:** Participants in family or group therapy often offer each other support, encouragement, and advice based on shared experiences. This mutual support reinforces the commitment to change and motivates them to overcome challenges associated with technology addiction.

6. **Technology Addiction Treatment Programs**

    1. **Inpatient Treatment Programs:** These programs offer intensive, round-the-clock care

within a treatment facility. They provide a structured environment away from technology, focusing on detoxification, therapy sessions, skill-building workshops, and mental health support. Inpatient programs are suitable for severe cases requiring comprehensive, immersive treatment.

2. **Outpatient Treatment Programs:** Outpatient programs allow individuals to receive treatment while living at home. They involve therapy sessions, support groups, and counseling scheduled at specific times. These programs offer flexibility for individuals with milder addiction or those who cannot commit to inpatient care due to personal or professional obligations.

3. **Residential Programs:** Residential programs combine elements of inpatient and outpatient care. Individuals reside in a supportive environment conducive to recovery while engaging in therapy, education, and skill-building activities. These programs offer a balance between structure and independence.

4. **Support Groups:** Various support groups, such as TechAddiction Anonymous or similar organizations, provide peer support and a platform for individuals to share experiences, strategies, and encouragement in managing technology addiction. These groups often follow a 12-step program and can be integral to ongoing recovery efforts.

5. **Digital Detox Retreats:** Retreats or camps specifically tailored for digital detoxification offer a break from technology in a supportive, therapeutic environment. They focus on mindfulness, outdoor activities, and self-reflection, providing participants with a reset from technology dependence.

6. **Therapeutic Boarding Schools:** For adolescents struggling with severe technology addiction, therapeutic boarding schools offer a structured environment with therapy, education, and activities that promote healthy habits, social skills, and academic progress while limiting technology access.

7. **Specialized Counseling Centers:** Some mental health centers or private practices specialize in treating technology addiction. They offer individualized therapy, counseling, and interventions tailored to address the unique challenges of technology dependency.

7. Counselling Strategies for Different Age Groups

1. Children (Under 12):

- **Play Therapy:** Utilizes play to communicate and express emotions, allowing children to explore feelings related to technology use indirectly.

- **Family-Based Approaches:** Involves parents to set boundaries, establish healthy habits, and encourage alternative activities that don't involve screens.

- **Education through Stories or Games:** Engages children in storytelling or gaming formats to impart knowledge about responsible technology use and potential risks.

2. **Adolescents (13-17):**

- **Cognitive-behavioral therapy (CBT):** Helps identify thought patterns and behaviors related to technology use, teaching coping mechanisms and problem-solving skills.

- **Group Therapy:** Offers peer support and allows adolescents to relate to others' experiences while learning healthy tech habits together.

- **Digital Literacy Programs:** Focuses on teaching critical thinking and responsible online behavior to navigate the digital world safely.

3. **Young Adults and Adults (18-65):**

- **Cognitive-Behavioral Therapy (CBT):** Continues to be effective, addressing deeper-rooted tech dependency issues and associated mental health concerns.

- **Mindfulness-Based Interventions:** Teaches stress reduction and self-awareness techniques to manage technology use and its impact on mental well-being.

- **Skill-Building Workshops:** Offers practical skills like time management, effective communication, and stress reduction to balance tech use.

4. **Elderly (65+):**

- **One-on-One Counseling:** Offers personalized sessions to address feelings of isolation due to technology, and educates on digital tools to enhance connection without dependency.

- **Technology Literacy Programs:** Focuses on teaching digital literacy at a pace suitable for older adults, reducing fear or intimidation toward technology while promoting safe usage.

- **Social Engagement Initiatives:** Encourages participation in community events, clubs, or groups to foster face-to-face interactions, reducing reliance on technology for socialization.

8. **Online Counselling and Teletherapy**

   Effectiveness of Online Counseling:

   1. **Accessibility:** Online counseling or teletherapy provides easier access to mental health professionals, overcoming geographical barriers or mobility issues.

   2. **Convenience:** Allows individuals to schedule sessions at their convenience, reducing time constraints and making therapy more accessible to those with busy schedules.

   3. **Anonymity and Comfort:** Provides a sense of anonymity, encouraging individuals who might feel uncomfortable or anxious in face-to-face settings to open up more freely.

   4. **Consistent Support:** Offers consistent support, especially in cases where individuals have difficulty committing to in-person

sessions regularly.

5. **Effective Communication:** Video calls can still convey non-verbal cues, enabling therapists to assess and address concerns effectively.

Availability of Online Counseling Services:

1. **Private Practitioners:** Many private therapists offer online counseling or teletherapy services through secure platforms.

2. **Mental Health Apps:** Several apps provide access to licensed therapists for text-based or video counseling sessions.

3. **Teletherapy Platforms:** Specialized platforms cater to teletherapy, connecting individuals with therapists specializing in technology addiction or related mental health concerns.

4. **Healthcare Providers:** Some healthcare providers or mental health institutions offer online counseling as part of their services.

Considerations:

1. **Security and Confidentiality:** Ensuring the platform used for teletherapy sessions is secure and complies with privacy regulations.

2. **Internet Connectivity:** A stable internet connection is crucial for uninterrupted sessions.

3. **Technology Literacy:** Ensuring individuals are comfortable using the technology required for online counseling.

4. **Emergency Situations:** Having a plan in place for emergencies or crises during online sessions.

Effectiveness Evaluation:

1. **Client Feedback:** Regular feedback from clients can gauge the effectiveness of online counseling sessions.

2. **Outcome Measures:** Tracking improvements in mental health and behavior through assessment tools.

3. **Therapist Perspective:** Evaluating the therapist's observations on the progress made during online sessions.

9. **Supportive Resources and Communities**

   Supportive Communities and Forums:

   1. **Online Communities:** Dedicated forums and communities provide a space for individuals to share experiences, seek advice, and find support from others facing similar challenges related to technology addiction.

   2. **Peer Support Groups:** Platforms offering peer-to-peer support, where individuals share strategies, stories, and encouragement while navigating technology addiction.

   3. **Specialized Forums:** Forums or groups specifically tailored to address various aspects of technology addiction, focusing on specific demographics or types of tech-related issues.

   4. **Moderated Spaces:** Platforms with moderators or professionals overseeing discussions to ensure a safe and supportive environment.

   Helplines and Hotlines:

   1. **Technology Addiction Hotlines:** Helplines specifically designated to offer support,

guidance, and resources for individuals grappling with technology addiction.

2. **Mental Health Hotlines:** General mental health helplines often provide assistance and referrals for those struggling with technology addiction's mental health impacts.

3. **24/7 Support:** Helplines available round-the-clock to offer immediate assistance or crisis intervention for individuals in distress due to technology addiction.

Professional Guidance and Referrals:

1. **Counseling Referrals:** Services offering guidance and referrals to licensed therapists or counselors specializing in technology addiction.

2. **Online Support Groups:** Virtual support groups hosted by mental health professionals to facilitate discussions and provide guidance on managing technology-related issues.

Interactive Online Resources:

1. **Educational Platforms:** Websites or portals offering educational resources, articles, and interactive tools to understand and manage technology addiction.

2. **Self-Help Modules:** Online modules or courses designed to assist individuals in addressing technology addiction through self-guided programs.

Community Engagement and Participation:

1. **Active Participation:** Encouragement for individuals to actively engage and participate

in discussions, seek advice, and contribute to the community.

2. **Information Sharing:** Platforms providing verified and up-to-date information about technology addiction, treatment options, and coping mechanisms.

Anonymity and Confidentiality:

1. **Anonymous Support:** Platforms ensuring anonymity or confidentiality for individuals who might be uncomfortable sharing personal information.

2. **Safe Spaces:** Creating safe and non-judgmental spaces where individuals feel comfortable sharing their experiences and seeking support.

10. Empowering Self-Help Techniques

Mindfulness and Relaxation Practices:

1. **Mindfulness Meditation:** Guidance on mindfulness exercises and meditation techniques to foster awareness and reduce compulsive tech usage.

2. **Breathing Exercises:** Techniques for deep breathing and relaxation to manage stress and anxiety associated with technology addiction.

Digital Well-being Apps and Tools:

1. **Time-Tracking Apps:** Applications that monitor screen time, helping individuals become aware of their digital habits and encouraging moderation.

2. **Focus Apps:** Tools designed to minimize distractions, promote focus, and limit access to certain apps or websites for set durations.

Behavioral Modification Strategies:

1. **Reward Systems:** Implementing personal reward systems for reducing screen time or achieving specific tech use goals.

2. **Habit Reversal Techniques:** Methods to identify triggers and replace excessive tech use habits with healthier alternatives.

Journaling and Self-Reflection:

1. **Daily Journaling:** Encouraging individuals to maintain a tech diary to track feelings, triggers, and thoughts associated with their technology use.

2. **Self-Reflection Exercises:** Prompts for self-reflection on the impact of technology on their lives, relationships, and mental health.

Digital Detox Practices:

1. **Scheduled Breaks:** Strategies for planned periods of digital detox, where individuals disconnect from devices for set durations.

2. **Unplugged Activities:** Recommendations for hobbies, outdoor pursuits, or creative endeavors to engage in during digital detox periods.

Establishing Healthy Routines:

1. **Sleep Hygiene Techniques:** Tips for maintaining a tech-free bedtime routine to improve sleep quality and overall well-being.

2. **Physical Activity Integration:** Guidance on incorporating physical exercise and movement into daily routines, reducing sedentary behavior associated with tech use.

Community Support and Online Forums:

1. **Peer Support Networks:** Encouragement to seek out and engage with online communities that provide peer support and understanding.

2. **Sharing Experiences:** Emphasis on the benefits of sharing experiences, strategies, and successes with others facing similar challenges.

11. Key Takeaways:

1. **Importance of Seeking Help:** Recognizing the signs indicating the need for professional assistance is crucial in managing technology addiction effectively.

2. **Diverse Therapeutic Options:** Understanding the range of therapeutic approaches available, including cognitive-behavioral therapy, group sessions, family therapy, and specialized treatment programs, empowers individuals to select the most fitting option.

3. **Tailored Counselling Strategies:** Addressing technology addiction requires customized approaches based on age groups, embracing the unique challenges faced by children, adolescents, adults, and the elderly.

4. **Online Counselling and Resources:** Accessibility to online counselling and teletherapy broadens the reach of support, offering convenient options for those seeking help.

5. **Empowerment through Self-Help:** Complementing professional therapy with self-help techniques, digital wellness apps, and

supportive communities empowers individuals to take an active role in their recovery journey.

6. **Encouragement to Seek Support:** Emphasizing the importance of seeking professional help and guidance, this chapter encourages individuals to explore available resources for effectively managing and overcoming technology addiction.

Chapter 11:

Rebuilding a Balanced Lifestyle Beyond Technology

1. **Introduction: Rebuilding a Balanced Lifestyle Beyond Technology**

In an era dominated by technology, regaining equilibrium in life beyond digital devices becomes paramount. This chapter serves as a guide to navigating the process of rediscovering a harmonious existence beyond the pervasive influence of technology.

Transitioning from Dependency: fosters

Transitioning away from technology dependency involves a multifaceted approach encompassing psychological, behavioral, and lifestyle changes. It's about reclaiming autonomy and rediscovering fulfillment beyond the digital realm.

Exploring Offline Fulfillment:

Delving into activities, hobbies, and experiences that nourish the soul beyond the confines of screens. This section emphasizes the importance of finding joy, purpose, and connection through offline endeavours.

Cultivating Real-Life Connections:

Rebuilding authentic, face-to-face connections and nurturing meaningful relationships outside the digital domain. Fostering genuine connections and intimacy becomes a cornerstone of a balanced lifestyle.

Mindful Tech Integration:

Strategically integrating technology into life without letting it dominate. Understanding the role of technology as a tool rather than the centrepiece of existence is crucial in achieving balance.

Embracing Slow Living:

Embracing a slower, more deliberate pace of life that allows for mindfulness, appreciation of the present moment, and a deeper connection with oneself and surroundings.

Reconnecting with Nature:

Highlighting the therapeutic effects of nature and advocating for reconnecting with the natural world to restore mental and emotional well-being.

Holistic Wellness Practices:

Exploring holistic wellness practices that encompass physical, mental, and emotional health beyond the digital sphere. Prioritizing self-care and adopting routines that promote overall well-being.

Strategies for Sustainable Change:

Offering strategies and tools to facilitate sustainable changes, promoting consistency and longevity in the pursuit of a balanced lifestyle.

2. Reassessing Priorities and Values

In a technologically saturated world, the chapter encourages a profound introspection into personal values and priorities. It prompts readers to evaluate the significance of digital engagement in their lives, inviting them to realign with their core values and aspirations.

Reflecting on Personal Values:

Encouraging readers to engage in introspective exercises that delve into what truly matters to them beyond the digital realm. This section assists in identifying and prioritizing values that may have been overshadowed by technology.

Aligning Actions with Aspirations:

Translating identified values into actionable goals and lifestyle changes. It involves crafting a plan to integrate these values into daily life, fostering a sense of purpose and fulfillment.

Mindful Consumption Habits:

Highlighting the importance of consciously consuming digital content in line with one's values. It involves curating digital experiences that enrich life and support the newly identified priorities.

Balancing Material and Experiential Pursuits:

Exploring the balance between material possessions and experiences. Encouraging readers to invest in experiences that resonate with their values, fostering personal growth and fulfillment.

Cultivating Emotional Intelligence:

Emphasizing the significance of emotional intelligence in navigating a life beyond technology. This section discusses the role of empathy, self-awareness, and social skills in enhancing relationships and fostering a fulfilling existence.

Holistic Life Planning:

Guiding readers through the process of developing holistic life plans that encompass personal, professional, and social aspects. Encouraging a balanced approach to goal-setting and lifestyle design.

Strategies for Lifestyle Alignment:

Offering strategies and techniques to align daily habits, routines, and decisions with identified values and priorities. This section provides actionable steps for readers to enact meaningful changes.

3. Exploring Offline Activities

Cultivating New Hobbies:

Encouraging readers to discover and delve into hobbies and activities that resonate with their interests, ranging from artistic pursuits like painting, sculpting, or writing to physical activities such as hiking, gardening, or sports.

Hands-On Creativity:

Promoting engagement in hands-on creative pursuits like crafting, DIY projects, woodworking, or cooking, fostering a sense of accomplishment and skill development.

Cultural and Artistic Engagement:

Encouraging exploration of cultural activities like visiting museums, attending live performances, exploring local art scenes, or joining book clubs, promoting intellectual stimulation and community engagement.

Nature Immersion:

Advocating spending time in nature, including activities like bird watching, camping, gardening, or nature photography, fostering a connection with the natural world, and promoting relaxation.

Physical Fitness and Well-being:

Promoting physical activities such as yoga, dance, team sports, or regular exercise routines, enhances overall health and mental well-being.

Community Involvement:

Encouraging involvement in community service, volunteering, or joining local clubs and organizations to foster social connections and contribute to a greater cause.

Mindfulness Practices:

Introducing mindfulness techniques like meditation, deep breathing exercises, or mindfulness walks, fostering self-awareness and promotes relaxation.

Educational Pursuits:

Encouraging continued learning through educational courses, workshops, or learning a new language, stimulating mental faculties, and supporting personal growth.

4. Nurturing Relationships

Quality Time with Family:

Encouraging dedicated family time through activities like family game nights, cooking together, storytelling, or simply sharing conversations, strengthening familial bonds and communication.

Deepening Friendships:

Exploring ways to strengthen friendships by organizing regular gatherings, going on outings, engaging in shared interests, or simply spending quality time together, nurturing meaningful connections.

Socializing Beyond Screens:

Advocating for face-to-face interactions with friends and peers by organizing social events, attending community gatherings, or participating in group activities, fostering genuine connections.

Networking and Community Building:

Encouraging involvement in local community events,

neighborhood gatherings, or social groups to expand social circles and build a supportive community network.

Communication and Active Listening:

Promoting effective communication techniques such as active listening, empathy, and understanding in interpersonal relationships, fostering deeper connections and mutual respect.

Conflict Resolution:

Discussing healthy conflict resolution strategies within relationships, emphasizing open communication, compromise, and understanding to resolve disagreements constructively.

Reconnecting with Nature:

Encouraging shared outdoor activities with friends or family like hiking, picnics, or nature walks, fosters a sense of togetherness and appreciation for the natural world.

Volunteering Together:

Promoting volunteer activities as a group or family unit, encouraging shared experiences that contribute to the community while strengthening relationships.

Celebrating Milestones:

Encouraging the celebration of important milestones, achievements, and special occasions with loved ones, fosters a sense of belonging and shared joy.

5. Embracing Mindfulness in Everyday Life

Mindful Daily Practices:

Morning Rituals:

Encouraging mindfulness upon waking by engaging in activities like meditation, setting intentions for the day, or practicing deep breathing exercises.

Mindful Eating:

Emphasizing mindful eating habits by savoring meals, paying attention to flavors and textures, and being present during the eating process without distractions.

Gratitude Journaling:

Promoting gratitude practices such as keeping a journal to jot down moments of gratitude, and fostering a positive mindset and appreciation for life's simple pleasures.

Mindful Movement:

Encouraging mindfulness through physical activities like yoga, tai chi, or mindful walking, focusing on the present moment and bodily sensations.

Stress Management Techniques:

Promoting stress reduction techniques like progressive muscle relaxation, visualization, or body scans, aiding in relaxation and stress relief.

Mindful Work Approach:

Encouraging mindfulness at work by taking regular breaks, practicing mindfulness during tasks, and fostering a focused and present mindset while working.

Mindful Communication:

Promoting mindful communication by actively listening, being present in conversations, and responding thoughtfully, fosters better understanding and connection in interactions.

Evening Reflection:

Encouraging reflection before bed, practicing mindfulness through gratitude exercises or meditation to unwind and prepare for restful sleep.

Mindful Observation:

Encouraging observation of surroundings, nature, or people

without judgment or analysis, fosters a sense of appreciation for the present moment.

6. Pursuing Physical and Mental Well-being

Physical Fitness:

Regular Exercise Routine:

Encouraging a consistent exercise regimen, incorporating activities like cardio, strength training, yoga, or any preferred physical activity to boost overall fitness.

Outdoor Activities:

Promoting engagement in outdoor activities like hiking, cycling, or nature walks to combine exercise with exposure to natural environments.

Healthy Eating Habits:

Encouraging a balanced diet with whole foods, adequate hydration, and mindful eating practices to support overall health and vitality.

Sleep Hygiene:

Emphasizing the importance of quality sleep by practicing good sleep hygiene, maintaining a regular sleep schedule, and creating a restful environment.

Stress Management:

Promoting stress-relief practices such as meditation, deep breathing exercises, or mindfulness to alleviate stress and promote mental well-being.

Mindfulness and Relaxation:

Encouraging activities that promote relaxation and mental rejuvenation, such as reading, hobbies, or engaging in creative pursuits.

Social Connection:

Fostering relationships and social interactions with friends, family, or communities to promote emotional well-being and a sense of belonging.

Mind-Body Practices:

Encouraging practices that link mental and physical health, such as tai chi, qi gong, or practices that integrate movement with mindfulness.

7. Rediscovering Creativity

Artistic Pursuits:

Encouraging engagement in art forms like drawing, painting, sculpting, or crafting to explore creativity and self-expression.

Writing and Journaling:

Promoting the practice of writing, whether it's creative writing, journaling, poetry, or storytelling, as a means of self-reflection and creative expression.

Music and Performing Arts:

Encouraging involvement in music—playing an instrument, singing, or exploring dance or theater—as a way to channel creative energy.

Photography or Visual Arts:

Exploring photography, videography, or any visual arts that involve capturing moments or expressing ideas through visual mediums.

Cooking and Culinary Arts:

Encouraging culinary exploration, experimenting with recipes, or creating meals as a form of creative expression and relaxation.

Gardening and Nature Exploration:

Promoting gardening or spending time outdoors, connecting with nature, and exploring creativity through landscaping or nature-inspired projects.

DIY and Home Projects:

Engaging in DIY projects, home improvement, or interior design as creative outlets to express individual tastes and styles.

8.   Setting Goals and Prioritizing Balance

Define Clear Goals:

Encourage individuals to set specific, measurable, achievable, relevant, and time-bound (SMART) goals that encompass various aspects of life, not solely related to technology.

Time Management Strategies:

Promote effective time management techniques, such as creating schedules, using productivity tools, and prioritizing tasks to allocate time for various activities.

Establishing Boundaries:

Encourage the setting of clear boundaries between personal and digital life, defining specific times or spaces for technology use and offline activities.

Creating a Balance Wheel:

Introduce the concept of a balance wheel, a visual representation of different life areas like work, family, health, hobbies, and spirituality, to assess and improve balance.

Regular Review and Adjustment:

Encourage individuals to periodically review their goals and schedules, adjusting them to ensure they align with evolving needs and priorities.

Practice Self-Care:

Highlight the importance of self-care activities like mindfulness, relaxation, and pursuing hobbies to maintain emotional and mental well-being.

9.   Sustainable Technology Use

Mindful Consumption:

Encourage intentional and mindful tech usage by fostering an awareness of the purpose behind each use and its impact on personal well-being.

Tech-Free Time:

Highlight the significance of allocating specific periods for tech-free activities, emphasizing the need for downtime away from screens.

Digital Minimalism:

Introduce the concept of digital minimalism, encouraging individuals to declutter their digital lives by reducing unnecessary apps, subscriptions, or digital clutter.

Setting Usage Limits:

Suggest setting limits on daily screen time or specific app usage to maintain a healthy balance between online and offline activities.

Mindful Engagement:

Encourage individuals to consciously engage with technology, avoiding mindless scrolling or excessive use by being selective about content consumption.

Prioritizing Real-Life Interactions:

Emphasize the importance of prioritizing face-to-face interactions over digital communication, especially in meaningful relationships.

10. Embracing Nature and Outdoor Activities

Nature's Healing:

Explore the therapeutic benefits of spending time in nature, including reduced stress, improved mood, and overall mental well-being.

Outdoor Pursuits:

Suggest outdoor activities such as hiking, gardening, cycling, or simply spending time in green spaces to promote physical exercise and mental relaxation.

Mindful Nature Immersion:

Encourage mindfulness while outdoors, urging individuals to engage their senses and be present in the natural environment to fully reap its benefits.

Tech-Free Outdoor Time:

Advocate for tech-free outdoor excursions to allow individuals to disconnect from screens and fully immerse themselves in the natural world.

Family and Community Outings:

Promote group activities or family outings in natural settings to foster social connections and a shared appreciation for the outdoors.

Sustainability Awareness:

Raise awareness about environmental sustainability and conservation, encouraging responsible outdoor practices to preserve nature.

11. Continual Assessment and Adaptation

Lifestyle Evaluation:

Encourage periodic self-assessment to evaluate habits, identifying areas that require adjustment or realignment.

Flexibility in Habits:

Advocate for flexible routines that can accommodate changes in personal circumstances while supporting overall well-being.

Learning from Experience:

Highlight the value of learning from past experiences, both successes and challenges, to refine lifestyle choices for better outcomes.

Openness to Change:

Encourage a mindset open to change, emphasizing that adjusting habits based on evolving needs is a sign of adaptability and growth.

Goal Reassessment:

Suggest revisiting personal goals regularly, ensuring they align with current aspirations and circumstances, and modifying them as needed.

Supportive Networks:

Promote seeking guidance and support from communities, mentors, or professionals to facilitate successful adaptation and growth.

12. Key Takeaways

Rebuilding Beyond Tech Dependency:

1. **Values and Priorities:** Reassess personal values to align with life goals beyond technology.

2. **Offline Engagement:** Explore diverse offline activities for personal growth and fulfillment.

3. **Relationship Building:** Foster meaningful connections with family, friends, and community offline.

4. **Mindfulness Integration:** Incorporate mindfulness practices into daily life for presence and gratitude.

5. **Well-being Focus:** Prioritize physical and mental health through exercise, nutrition, and mental well-being practices.

6. **Creativity Rediscovery:** Encourage creative expression through non-digital mediums for self-expression.

7. **Balanced Living:** Set achievable goals, establish boundaries, and manage time for a balanced lifestyle.

8. **Responsible Tech Use:** Integrate healthy tech habits without overreliance, supporting moderation.

9. **Nature Connection:** Embrace outdoor activities and nature to reap their benefits for well-being.

10. **Continual Adaptation:** Encourage continual assessment and adaptation to evolving circumstances for sustained balance.

V.

Moving Forward

Chapter 12:

The Future of Technology and Healthy Interaction

1. Introduction

"Navigating Tomorrow's Digital Terrain: Cultivating Healthy Bonds with Technology"

The future beckons with promises of technological marvels, inviting us into an era where innovation and human existence intertwine more intimately than ever. As we stand on the precipice of this technological revolution, the quest for a balanced and symbiotic relationship between humanity and technology has never been more pertinent.

In this final chapter, we embark on a visionary journey into the heart of tomorrow's technological landscape. We navigate the uncharted waters where artificial intelligence, augmented realities, and unparalleled connectivity redefine the fabric of human existence. As technology evolves, so too must our relationship with it. It's an age where fostering a healthy equilibrium between digital innovation and mindful interaction becomes imperative.

The narrative transcends a mere observation of cutting-edge advancements; it becomes a testament to the need for intentional and balanced cohabitation with technology. Here, we scrutinize the seeds of healthy digital interaction planted today to yield a harmonious tomorrow. It's a call to action, an invitation to sculpt a future where technology enriches our lives without compromising our well-being.

In these digital musings lies a roadmap, a blueprint for the future generation to forge a path where the brilliance of technology coalesces seamlessly with the essence of human existence. As the curtain rises on the future of technology, it's our collective responsibility to shape a narrative that cherishes innovation while safeguarding our humanity.

2. Technological Advancements

"Tomorrow's Tapestry: Technological Advances and Human Interplay"

In the tapestry of technological evolution, tomorrow's threads are woven with the promises of advancements that transcend imagination. The corridors of innovation echo the strides taken by artificial intelligence, augmented reality, and virtual landscapes, heralding a paradigm shift in our interaction with the digital realm.

This chapter is an exploration of these imminent advancements, a journey into the fertile grounds where technology and human behavior intersect. From the poised evolution of artificial intelligence, where machines echo human cognition, to the immersive realms of augmented and virtual realities that redefine our sensory experiences, these advancements encapsulate the extraordinary.

As these technologies burgeon, they cast an intricate web, intertwining with the very fabric of our lives. They beckon us toward unprecedented interactions, promising transformation in education, work, entertainment, and daily engagement. Yet, within this promise lies a potential crossroads – one that mandates a cautious understanding of how these technological leaps might influence our psyche, behavior, and interpersonal connections.

This chapter is not just a canvas of tomorrow's innovations; it's an inquiry into the potential impact of these advancements on the human landscape. It's a quest to discern the fine balance between embracing progress and safeguarding the essence of genuine human connection. As these innovations march toward the horizon, it becomes our collective responsibility to guide their trajectory toward a future where technological brilliance aligns harmoniously with the preservation of human values and well-being.

3.   Balancing Innovation and Well-being

"The Balancing Act: Nurturing Innovation while Safeguarding Well-being"

Innovation is the harbinger of progress, etching new frontiers and reshaping human existence. Yet, amidst the kaleidoscope of technological marvels, lies an intricate dance between innovation's ceaseless stride and the sanctity of human well-being. This chapter delves into the intricate interplay between technological advancement and the imperative call to safeguard mental health and ethical considerations.

The challenge lies not in stifling innovation but in sculpting its trajectory with an ethical compass, nurturing its growth while safeguarding the human essence. It's a call to action – a harmonious integration of groundbreaking innovation and ethical responsibility.

Ethical considerations are the cornerstone of this discourse. As technology propels forward, ethical boundaries must pave the path, steering innovation toward societal benefit without compromising individual well-being. Exploring the nexus of responsibility and innovation, this chapter contemplates the ethical nuances that underpin the ever-evolving tech landscape.

Beyond ethics, the heart of this exploration is the preservation of mental health. Innovation's magnetic allure often leads to a digital whirlwind, challenging the delicate balance of mental well-being. From addictive interfaces to intrusive data practices, this chapter scrutinizes the psychological impact of technological advancements, shedding light on how responsible innovation can bolster mental resilience rather than erode it.

This chapter is a quest for equilibrium – a testament to the possibility of thriving technological progress while ensuring the sanctity of human dignity, mental health, and ethical integrity. It's a symphony where innovation and responsibility converge, crafting a future where the marvels of technology stand hand in hand with the nurturing of human well-being.

4. Human-Centered Design

"Designing for Humanity: Human-Centered Technology for Well-being"

- Innovation isn't solely about technological breakthroughs; it's about the people it serves. Enter human-centered design – the pivot point where technology transcends mere functionality to embrace empathy and user-centricity.

- This chapter is a voyage into the essence of human-centered design, where the pulse of innovation beats in harmony with the needs, aspirations, and well-being of its users. At its core lies the recognition that technology isn't an end in itself but a tool to enhance lives. Here, we explore how this approach can revolutionize the landscape of tech addiction.

- In an era where screen time is measured not just

in hours but in its impact on mental health, human-centered design emerges as a guiding beacon. It's a call to craft interfaces, apps, and platforms that don't merely captivate but elevate, promoting healthy digital interaction rather than ensnaring users in addictive loops.

- This chapter unpacks the core tenets of human-centered design and its transformative power in mitigating addictive behaviors. Through real-world examples and expert insights, it illuminates how technology can be a force for good, fostering a symbiotic relationship where user well-being flourishes in tandem with technological innovation.

- It's a paradigm shift – a journey where technology bends not just to the whims of innovation but bows gracefully to the sanctity of human experience. This chapter is an ode to the union of technology and empathy, a testament to a future where innovation breathes life into well-being, guided by the wisdom of human-centered design.

5. Digital Wellness and Mindful Tech Adoption

"Navigating the Digital Oasis: Embracing Digital Wellness for Mindful Tech Adoption"

The digital landscape is evolving, not just in its innovations but in its conscience. Enter the era of digital wellness – a movement dedicated to fostering a healthier relationship with technology. This chapter is an exploration of this burgeoning domain, where digital tools aren't just about utility but about nurturing a mindful and balanced tech lifestyle.

In this chapter, we embark on a journey through the realms of digital wellness, illuminating the emergence of tools, features, and initiatives meticulously crafted to promote mindful tech adoption. From apps nudging users towards healthier habits to platforms fostering digital detox, we traverse the spectrum of interventions designed to infuse consciousness into digital interactions.

We delve into the core of digital wellness initiatives, uncovering their impact on user behavior and mental well-being. How do these tools gently guide users towards mindful tech habits? What strategies do they employ to strike a balance between engagement and disconnection?

Through expert insights and user experiences, this chapter illuminates the practicality and efficacy of digital wellness tools in encouraging conscious tech use. It's a tapestry woven with stories of individuals who found solace in the digital wellness realm, transforming their relationship with technology from one of dependency to one of empowerment.

This chapter is a testament to the metamorphosis underway in the tech sphere – a shift from mindless scrolling to purposeful interaction. It's an invitation to embrace digital wellness as a beacon guiding us to a future where technology augments our lives, fostering well-being and mindfulness in the digital oasis.

6. Education and Digital Literacy

"Empowering Through Knowledge: Fostering Digital Literacy for Responsible Tech Navigation"

- In an age where technology is ubiquitous, understanding its nuances and wielding it responsibly is paramount. This chapter is an exploration of the cornerstone that fortifies our digital existence: digital literacy and education.

- Here, we embark on an insightful journey

elucidating the criticality of digital literacy in nurturing responsible tech use. We navigate the complex landscape of the digital world, emphasizing that knowledge is the compass that guides us through its intricacies.

- This chapter unpacks the importance of digital literacy as more than just the ability to use digital tools but as the mastery of navigating the digital terrain. We shine a light on strategies and initiatives aimed at bolstering digital literacy, empowering individuals to wield technology as a tool for growth and productivity, not mere consumption.

- Through expert insights and user experiences, we illustrate the transformative power of digital education. How does it equip individuals to discern between reliable information and misinformation? How does it arm users with the critical thinking skills necessary to navigate the vast digital realm?

- This chapter invites readers to embrace digital literacy not just as a skill set but as a superpower, empowering individuals to navigate the digital universe with confidence and responsibility. It's a testament to the profound impact of education in shaping responsible tech users and fostering a safer, more informed digital society.

7. Cultivating Technological Mindfulness

"Technological Mindfulness: Balancing Presence in a Digital World"

In the ever-evolving landscape of technology, mindfulness

emerges as a beacon guiding us toward balanced and purposeful tech engagement. This chapter embarks on a journey through the synergy between mindfulness practices and our digital existence.

Here, we unravel the profound influence of mindfulness on our technological interactions. We explore how the practice of mindfulness, rooted in awareness and intentional presence, serves as a potent antidote to the siren call of addictive tech behaviors. Through expert perspectives and user narratives, we showcase how mindfulness empowers individuals to navigate the digital labyrinth consciously, fostering healthy relationships with technology.

Delving deeper, we delve into the innovative integration of mindfulness practices within digital interfaces. How can technology itself become a catalyst for mindfulness? We explore the burgeoning landscape of apps, interfaces, and digital tools engineered to nudge users toward mindful engagement, promoting pauses for reflection in a world of incessant digital noise.

This chapter isn't merely an exploration of mindfulness; it's a testament to its transformative power in the digital sphere. It's an invitation to infuse intentionality into our tech-driven lives, fostering a harmonious relationship between humans and technology—one anchored in mindfulness and purposeful engagement.

8. Humanizing Technology

"Humanizing Technology: Nurturing Empathy in Digital Interactions"

- This chapter invites readers into the realm of technology reimagined—an era where empathy and human connection converge with innovation. Here, we explore the evolving landscape of technology through the lens of emotional intelligence and human-centered design.

- The concept of humanizing technology transcends mere functionality; it's about infusing our digital creations with the warmth and understanding inherent in human interactions. We unravel initiatives and breakthroughs that prioritize emotional intelligence in tech design. How can technology not only serve but also empathize? We dive into the initiatives where technology acts as a conduit for fostering genuine emotional connections, bridging the gap between humans and machines.

- Through insightful discussions and real-world examples, we shed light on the revolutionary impact of human-centered design in technology. From AI-driven emotional companions to interfaces that understand and respond to human emotions, we traverse the forefront of tech innovation aiming not just to function but to understand and empathize.

- This chapter serves as an ode to the symbiotic relationship between technology and empathy. It's a testament to the transformative potential of human-centered tech initiatives, inspiring a new era where technology doesn't merely serve but empathizes and connects on a deeply human level.

9. Community and Social Engagement

"Tech's Role in Social Fabric: Fostering Genuine Community Engagement"

- This chapter unravels the intricate relationship between technology and authentic social interactions. We delve into how technology, when wielded mindfully, becomes a catalyst for community building rather than a substitute for genuine connections.

- We embark on a journey exploring the multifaceted roles technology plays in nurturing communities. From fostering connections in remote settings to amplifying local engagements, we examine platforms and initiatives that breathe life into community networks.

- Technology is not just about connecting people; it's about enhancing the richness of these connections. We dive into case studies and innovative platforms that enrich social engagements, discussing how digital spaces can mirror and support real-world communities.

- But it's not just about the digital realm replacing the physical. This chapter highlights the importance of preserving face-to-face interactions while harnessing technology as a tool to augment these connections. We explore ways technology can complement, rather than supplant, the authenticity of in-person engagements.

- Join us as we unravel the intricate balance between technology and community, where the digital landscape doesn't replace genuine connections but rather serves as a conduit for fostering, enhancing, and sustaining vibrant communities.

10. Responsible Tech Policies and Advocacy

"Tech Advocacy and Policy: Championing Ethical Tech Practices"

This chapter serves as a beacon illuminating the critical need for responsible tech policies and advocacy initiatives. It navigates through the labyrinth of ethical considerations, exploring how policy-making and advocacy can steer technology toward a more responsible and humane direction.

We delve into the landscape of tech policy-making, unraveling the complexities of crafting regulations that balance innovation with user well-being. This chapter examines the ethical frameworks and initiatives driving conversations around responsible tech practices globally.

Through case studies and expert insights, we illuminate the role of advocacy groups, governmental bodies, and grassroots movements in shaping policies that prioritize user privacy, data ethics, and digital well-being. We explore how these entities champion the cause for ethical tech practices and advocate for regulations that safeguard user interests.

Furthermore, we discuss the evolving nature of tech regulations in a dynamic landscape. How can policies keep pace with technological advancements? How do we ensure these policies remain adaptive and inclusive?

Join us as we dissect the nexus between responsible tech policies, advocacy efforts, and the imperative role they play in shaping the future of technology for the betterment of society.

11. The Role of Mental Health Professionals

"The Evolving Role of Mental Health Professionals in a Tech-Driven World"

- In this segment, we shed light on the pivotal role mental health professionals play in navigating the complex labyrinth of technology addiction and fostering mindful tech consumption. We explore their evolving responsibilities and approaches in the face of rapidly changing tech landscapes.

- **Understanding Changing Dynamics:** Discuss the changing dynamics in mental health practices due to the pervasive influence of technology. Explore how therapists and counselors adapt their methodologies to address emerging concerns related to excessive tech use, addiction, and its psychological ramifications.

- **Adapting Therapeutic Strategies:** Delve into the strategies mental health professionals employ to tackle technology addiction. From integrating digital detox therapies to mindfulness-based interventions, uncover how therapists tailor their approaches to help individuals regain control over their tech habits and enhance digital well-being.

- **The Collaborative Role:** Highlight the collaborative efforts between tech experts and mental health professionals. Discuss how interdisciplinary collaboration fosters innovative approaches to combat tech addiction, emphasizing the importance of cohesive efforts in addressing these challenges.

- **Education and Guidance:** Explore the role of mental health professionals in educating individuals about responsible tech usage. Discuss guidance strategies that therapists and counselors offer to promote digital literacy, mindful tech engagement, and a healthy balance between the digital and physical worlds.

- **Ethical Considerations:** Address the ethical responsibilities mental health professionals bear when dealing with tech-related issues. Discuss confidentiality, privacy concerns, and ethical boundaries in the digital therapy space.

- This section aims to showcase the evolving landscape of mental health practices in response to technology's impact. It emphasizes the adaptation, collaboration, and guidance provided by mental health professionals in navigating the complexities of tech-related challenges for improved digital well-being.

12. Preparing for the Future

"Preparing for a Healthy Tech Future"

- **Reflection on Insights:** Summarize key insights gleaned from the preceding discussions. Reflect on the multifaceted strategies, expert insights, and societal responsibilities highlighted throughout the chapter.

- **Individual Readiness:** Offer recommendations for individuals to embrace a future of healthy tech interaction. Encourage mindfulness, digital literacy, and the adoption of balanced tech habits. Emphasize the importance of self-awareness, setting boundaries, and seeking support when needed.

- **Societal Evolution:** Discuss the societal role in shaping a healthy tech future. Advocate for the cultivation of digital literacy programs in education systems, the formulation of responsible tech policies, and the integration of ethical considerations into tech design.

- **Human-Tech Symbiosis:** Propose strategies for fostering a harmonious relationship between humans and technology. Encourage the concept of technology as a tool for empowerment rather than dependency. Highlight the importance of designing tech that respects human well-being and augments our capabilities without compromising our humanity.

- **Embracing Change:** Encourage adaptability and a forward-thinking mindset. Stress the inevitability of technological evolution and the necessity to embrace change. Advocate for an ongoing dialogue between all stakeholders—tech developers, policymakers, mental health professionals, and individuals—to navigate future tech landscapes responsibly.

- This closing section aims to encapsulate the key takeaways, recommendations, and proactive measures required at both individual and societal levels to navigate a future where technology and humanity coexist harmoniously.

13. Key Takeaways

- **Individual Empowerment:** Individuals should embrace digital literacy, mindfulness, and balanced tech habits. Self-awareness, setting boundaries, and seeking support are crucial for healthy tech use.

- **Societal Responsibility:** Society plays a pivotal role in fostering a healthy tech future. It involves advocating for digital literacy programs, formulating responsible tech policies, and integrating ethical considerations into tech design.

- **Human-Tech Harmony:** Striving for a symbiotic relationship between humans and technology is vital. Technology should empower without fostering dependency. Prioritizing tech that respects well-being and augments human capabilities is essential.

- **Adapting to Change:** Embracing adaptability and forward-thinking is crucial. Acknowledging the inevitability of tech evolution, ongoing dialogues between stakeholders are necessary for responsible navigation of future tech landscapes.

- **Proactive Approach:** Encouraging a proactive stance toward tech usage ensures a healthy balance. Emphasizing responsible tech consumption, fostering digital literacy, and advocating for ethical tech practices are foundational.

These takeaways underscore the importance of proactively shaping a future where technology promotes well-being and responsible interaction, both at an individual and societal level

Chapter 13:

Conclusion: Finding Balance in a Digital World

1. Reflecting on the Journey

Introduction to Reflection • Begin by expressing gratitude for the exploration and insights gathered throughout the book, acknowledging the importance of the journey towards understanding technology's impact.

Recap of Key Themes • Summarize the central themes discussed in the book, such as technology addiction, psychological impacts, mindfulness, healthy tech habits, and the future of tech-human interaction.

Journey to Awareness • Discuss how the book aimed to raise awareness about the complexities of technology addiction, shedding light on its psychological, social, and physical implications.

Empowerment Through Knowledge • Highlight how knowledge empowers individuals to navigate the digital world more consciously, emphasizing the importance of mindfulness and informed tech use.

Recovery and Resilience • Reflect on stories of recovery, resilience, and the journeys of individuals overcoming technology addiction, showcasing hope and the potential for change.

Promoting Healthy Tech Interaction • Emphasize the

significance of promoting a balanced approach to tech use, encouraging mindfulness, setting boundaries, and fostering a healthy relationship with technology.

Looking to the Future • Discuss the importance of continuous learning, adaptation, and collaboration in shaping a future where technology enhances well-being without compromising it.

Call to Action • Encourage readers to apply the knowledge gained from the book, adopt healthier tech habits, seek support when needed, and contribute to a more mindful digital world.

Closing Thoughts • End with a note of encouragement, gratitude for the journey shared, and optimism for a future where technology and humanity coexist harmoniously.

Conclusion chapters serve as a poignant reminder of the key takeaways, emphasizing their application in everyday life and looking ahead to a future where technology enriches lives in a balanced and mindful manner.

14. Acknowledging the Challenges

Acknowledging the Struggles • Start by acknowledging the difficulties individuals encounter in navigating the omnipresence of technology in modern life, recognizing the allure and challenges it poses.

Impact on Mental Health • Discuss the profound impact of excessive tech use on mental health, referencing the discussed psychological effects, addiction tendencies, and emotional repercussions.

Pressures of the Digital Era • Address the societal pressures and expectations amplified by the digital era, such as the constant connectivity, FOMO (fear of missing out), and the demand for instant gratification.

Finding Balance in Complexity • Emphasize that finding balance in such a complex technological landscape is challenging but essential for well-being, underscoring the importance of the journey toward balance.

Empowering Through Understanding • Highlight how understanding the challenges is the first step toward managing them, empowering individuals to make informed decisions about their tech consumption.

Encouragement and Support • Offer words of encouragement, stressing that despite the challenges, support systems, knowledge, and mindfulness techniques discussed in the book can aid in navigating these difficulties.

The goal is to acknowledge the struggles while reinforcing the empowerment gained through knowledge and mindfulness techniques to combat these challenges effectively.

15. Embracing the Potential

Harnessing Technology's Potential • Acknowledge the transformative power of technology, citing its positive contributions to communication, education, healthcare, and social progress.

Innovation and Advancements • Highlight the impressive innovations technology has brought forth, revolutionizing industries, improving efficiency, and fostering global connectivity.

Empowerment and Opportunities • Discuss how technology has empowered individuals, providing access to information, opportunities for learning, and platforms for creative expression.

Balancing Potential with Responsibility • Emphasize the need to balance the positive aspects with responsible usage, underscoring the importance of mindful consumption and ethical tech practices.

Acknowledging the positive impacts, allows for a balanced perspective, advocating for responsible and mindful tech usage while appreciating the advancements and opportunities it brings to our lives.

16. The Importance of Awareness

The Power of Awareness • Emphasize how awareness serves as a cornerstone in recognizing and addressing technology addiction, urging individuals to stay mindful of their digital habits.

Mindful Tech Consumption • Encourage readers to maintain mindfulness in their tech usage, advocating for conscious engagement and regular self-assessment of their digital behaviors.

Empowerment Through Awareness • Highlight how being aware of technology's impact empowers individuals to make informed choices, enabling them to balance their digital lives for improved well-being.

Sustaining Mindful Habits • Stress the importance of continual awareness, urging readers to sustain mindful habits and regularly assess their relationship with technology for a more balanced lifestyle.

17. Empowerment through Knowledge

Harnessing Empowerment through Knowledge • Highlight how understanding the impact of technology on mental health equips individuals with the tools to navigate and control their digital engagements effectively.

Ownership of Tech Habits • Encourage readers to take ownership of their tech habits by leveraging the knowledge gained from the book, empowering them to make informed decisions for their well-being.

Transformative Knowledge • Emphasize how knowledge transforms passive users into conscious consumers, giving them agency to cultivate healthier relationships with technology for a more balanced life.

18. Striving for Balance

Striking the Balance • Emphasize the significance of finding equilibrium between digital engagements and offline activities, promoting a well-rounded lifestyle. • Encourage readers to consciously allocate time for tech use while prioritizing activities that nurture personal growth, relationships, and well-being.

Prioritizing Well-being • Highlight the importance of prioritizing mental and emotional well-being by consciously managing tech consumption and allocating time to activities that foster personal fulfillment and growth.

19. Moving Forward with Intent

- Moving Forward with Intent • Provide practical strategies for readers to implement gradual changes in their tech habits, such as scheduling tech-free hours, setting device usage limits, and practicing mindful consumption. • Encourage readers to establish clear intentions and achievable goals related to their tech habits, emphasizing the importance of consistency in creating lasting changes.

20. Continued Support and Growth

Continued Support and Growth • Emphasize the significance of ongoing support networks, such as support groups, therapists, or online communities, to sustain healthy tech habits and navigate challenges. • Encourage a mindset of continual growth and adaptation, advocating for regular reflection and adjustment in tech habits to align with evolving needs and goals.

21. The Journey Ahead

- The Journey Ahead: Navigating the Path to Balance As we conclude this exploration of technology and its impact on our lives, it's crucial to acknowledge that achieving a balanced relationship with technology is an ongoing journey rather than a destination. This journey entails consistent self-assessment, reflection, and a willingness to adapt to the ever-evolving digital landscape.

- Continuous Self-Reflection: Emphasize the importance of ongoing self-reflection in understanding our tech habits, motivations, and the impact they have on our overall well-being. Encourage readers to regularly assess their relationship with technology, considering how it aligns with their values and goals.

- Adaptability to Change: Highlight the need to stay adaptable in the face of technological advancements. Discuss how new innovations may influence our habits and routines, and encourage readers to embrace change while remaining mindful of its impact on their lives.

- Personal Growth: Encourage readers to view their tech habits as a part of their personal growth journey. Suggests that each individual's relationship with technology is unique and that growth may involve experimenting with different approaches to find what works best for them.

- Tech as a Tool for Growth: Discuss the positive potential of technology as a tool for personal growth and development. Encourage readers to explore how technology can facilitate learning, creativity, and connection when used intentionally and mindfully.

- Building Resilience: Highlight the importance of resilience in managing tech use. Discuss how setbacks or challenges in maintaining a balanced relationship with technology can be learning opportunities, fostering resilience and adaptability.

- Seeking Support: Reinforce the value of seeking support, whether through communities, professionals, or self-help resources. Encourage readers to continue seeking guidance and assistance whenever needed.

- Embracing the Process: Encourage readers to embrace the process of change and growth, emphasizing that a balanced relationship with technology is not a fixed state but rather an ongoing journey. Invite them to celebrate their progress while being patient with setbacks.

- In conclusion, the journey toward a balanced relationship with technology is a continual process of self-discovery and adaptation. Encourage readers to approach this journey with curiosity, openness, and a commitment to their well-being, knowing that each step forward contributes to a healthier and more mindful interaction with technology.

22. Final Thoughts

As we conclude this journey through the digital landscape, the quest for balance emerges as both a challenge and an empowering opportunity. Our relationship with technology is a dynamic journey, constantly evolving and demanding our conscious attention.

Embrace the Journey: Consider this not an endpoint, but a milestone in an ongoing journey towards mindful tech engagement. Recognize that every step taken towards balance is a triumph—a testament to your dedication to a more intentional and fulfilling life.

Optimism in Purpose: In the midst of this digital age, maintain an unwavering optimism. Your awareness and intentionality equip you to shape a future where technology serves as a facilitator, not a detractor, in your pursuit of a balanced life.

Champion Mindful Choices: Embrace the power vested in your choices. Every mindful decision regarding technology is a statement—a declaration of your commitment to a life rich in experiences, connections, and personal growth.

The Rhythm of Change: Embrace change as an ally on this path. Understand that adaptability is not a concession; it's an asset. Your flexibility and openness to change ensure that your relationship with technology evolves in sync with your evolving aspirations.

Elevating Well-being: Elevate your well-being as the cornerstone of your digital interactions. Prioritize moments of presence, nurture connections beyond screens, and cherish the real-world experiences that bring depth to your life.

A Call to Empowerment: The power lies within your grasp. Empower yourself with the knowledge gained, and carry forward this journey with a commitment to continual self-assessment and deliberate choices.

In closing, let each action and decision echo your commitment to a life anchored in balance and intentionality. The digital world is yours to navigate—forge ahead with purpose, mindfulness, and an unwavering commitment to a life well-lived.

23. Conclusion:

In the tapestry of our digital landscape, the ancient wisdom of "Vasudhaiva Kutumbakam" resonates more profoundly than ever before. As we conclude our exploration into digital harmony, we find ourselves standing at the crossroads of technology and humanity, guided by the eternal truth that the world is indeed one family.

Our journey through the complexities of a wired world has illuminated the interconnectedness that defines our global existence. Every click, swipe, and interaction transcends geographical borders, binding us in a shared narrative where our digital footprints leave indelible marks on the fabric of our collective consciousness.

"Vasudhaiva Kutumbakam" beckons us to acknowledge this profound interdependence, urging us to reimagine our relationship with technology as a catalyst for unity and balance. In our pursuit of digital harmony, we're challenged not only to navigate the digital labyrinth but to weave threads of compassion, empathy, and responsibility into every digital interaction.

The ethos of this ancient philosophy invites us to embrace our role as global citizens in the digital age, to recognize that our actions in the virtual realm reverberate across continents, shaping the very essence of our shared human experience.

As we seek equilibrium amidst the whirlwind of technological advancements, let us carry the guiding principle of "Vasudhaiva Kutumbakam" as a beacon of mindful engagement. Let our interactions with technology reflect the unity, compassion, and understanding that define us as a single global family.

In cultivating digital harmony, may we not only find balance within ourselves but also extend a compassionate hand to others, fostering a world where technology becomes a bridge that unites rather than divides.

Let this philosophy infuse every aspect of our digital lives, nurturing a future where the principles of oneness and interconnectedness guide our technological evolution. Together, let us harmonize the digital symphony, embracing the unity that transcends screens and wires, and celebrating the profound truth that indeed, the world is one family.

24. Closing Remarks

As we draw the curtains on this exploration of our digital existence, let's reflect on the essence of our journey. Throughout these pages, we've delved into the intricate web of our relationship with technology, unearthing its impacts on our minds, our well-being, and our lives.

At its core, this book is a testament to the pursuit of balance—a quest for equilibrium in a world teeming with digital marvels. It's a call to action, urging us all to be mindful custodians of our tech habits and champions of harmonious coexistence with the digital realm.

To each reader who embarked on this insightful journey, I extend my heartfelt gratitude. Your curiosity, your openness to learning, and your commitment to a healthier tech-life balance have fueled this exploration. Your presence on this voyage has enriched its essence.

Remember, the essence of balance lies not in complete

abstinence but in intentional engagement—a delicate dance between the allure of technology and the enriching facets of the offline world. As we bid adieu, let's carry forth this wisdom and embark on our individual odysseys toward a more balanced, mindful, and fulfilling digital future.

Thank you for your companionship on this thought-provoking journey. May your pursuit of balance in the digital age be fruitful and your path enlightened with conscious choices.